The Energy Poker Game

THE ENERGY POKER GAME

The Politics of the Continental

Resources Deal

by James Laxer

new press/Toronto/Chicago 1970

ISBN 0-88770-031-4 (paperbound)

new press
84 Sussex Avenue
Toronto Canada

300 West Adams
Chicago Illinois 60606 U.S.A.

CONTENTS

i INTRODUCTION

It has been our fate in this century to be absorbed increasingly into the American empire, to be dominated in virtually every aspect of our lives by giant American-based corporations. But now, in the last third of the century, it is ever more evident that our destiny lies in struggling against that absorption, in calling a halt in the name of the Canadian people and beginning to build a new Canada that is independent, democratic and socialist.

No issue is today more central to the meaningful survival of Canada as a separate nation on this continent than who shall own and control our energy resources. Shall they be used to provide the basis for more jobs for Canadian workers? Shall Canadians as consumers get the benefits of the lower prices that might reasonably be expected to go with expanding supplies? Shall these resources be used so that further ecological and environmental damage is minimized? Shall they be owned by the people so that the surpluses inherent in resource development go to the many? Or will their development take place, as it has in the past, in the hands of profit-seeking corporations, with most of the benefits going to foreign corporations and their shareholders?

For let no one imagine that merely selling our unprocessed resources to foreigners, no matter how skillfully the price is negotiated, has in the past or will in the future provide any substantial benefits for ordinary Canadians. The Trudeau government as it skates away from its own White Paper lacks the sense even to tax the profits of resource corporations at the same level as other corporations! Higher export prices will mean simply higher profits for foreign shareholders and higher prices for Canadian consumers.

The questions I have put are those with which this book is concerned. It has been written under the pressure of time, for the hour is late. Indeed, as I sit writing these words, I read in the newspaper that American and Canadian officials are meeting behind closed doors in Montreal, apparently to negotiate a continental energy deal. But in spite of its brevity, this book admirably summarizes the key issues that must concern us and begins the difficult but essential task of working out an alternative strategy for an independent Canada. And it includes excerpts from key documents; if J. J. Green's off-again-on-again nationalism doesn't boggle your mind, perhaps the cool surrealism of the Shultz report will. For if Mr. Greene's antics do not insult your intelligence, the way the Shultz Report sees us as the safest place on earth from which to get the resources the U.S. needs to feed its war machine may insult your sensitivities.

James Laxer is eminently qualified to undertake the task of ringing the fire alarm. A brilliant young historian now teaching at Queen's University, he was a co-author of the Waffle Manifesto "For An Independent Socialist Canada". That Manifesto, and the national debate it triggered off has forced the Liberal Government to begin, albeit feebly, to come to grips with the problem of foreign ownership. Let us hope that this book is equally successful in forcing a Canada-wide debate on the continental energy deal into which this country is quietly drifting.

Tommy Douglas has called for a full debate in Parliament before a further step is taken down this disastrous course. It is uncertain as I write that Trudeau will see fit to accord us even this. What the Waffle Movement of the NDP is calling for, are demostrations, rallies and marches across Canada that will force the Government to cease and desist. We will be armed with this book. Read it and join us.

Mel Watkins
September 10, 1970

I THE ENERGY CRISIS - 1970

In December 1969, J. J. Greene, Canada's Minister of Energy, Mines and Resources, paid a visit to Washington. Following his lengthy discussions with U. S. Interior Secretary Walter Hickel, Greene made his now — famous observations in favour of a continental energy resources deal so that "people will benefit, and both countries will benefit, irrespective of where the imaginary border goes." Greene's cracker-barrel continentalism created a sensation in Canada.

Since that time there has been much speculation about what a continental energy resources deal would include and about whether, indeed, such a deal is imminent. The Canadian government has changed its emphasis from time to time since the first discussion of the energy deal. Negotiations on the subject have been proceeding, off and on with the Americans, we are told. The issue has been clouded in uncertainty as to its content and, as with most vital political questions in Canada, there has been only faint-hearted debate on the subject among the politicians.

In its most basic terms, a continental energy resources deal means the creation of a free North American market in energy resources. Present ownership and marketing patterns would be guaranteed a permanent existence, with the Canadian-American border erased in matters of energy resources This means secure and permanent access by American industry to Canadian energy resources and a guarantee that nothing would ever be done to interfere with that access whatever Canadian needs might become in the future. It involves a basic commitment by the Canadian government to regard this country's energy resources as continental resources, and to give up any plans it might have for the development of those energy resources outside the framework of American corporate and military interests.

Such a deal which would begin with natural gas, oil, electric power, coal and nuclear energy, might eventually be extended to include water. Whether concluded as a package or more likely piecemeal, the deal has vast implications for the future of the Canadian people. The deal is on our government's agenda at this moment.

The proposed continental free market in energy resources is similar to policies pursued by our government in the past. It is the natural extension of such policies. Many will ask what is so remarkable about this further step toward integration of the Canadian and American economies. The difference is that with the energy deal we cross a threshold in our relations with the United States that will be extremely difficult to recross. The energy deal will affect the future scope of the Canadian economy and will have a great impact on the number and kinds of jobs that will be available for Canadians in their own country. It will vitally affect our efforts to clean up the Canadian environment and to protect the ecological system, particularly in the Canadian north. Furthermore, it will greatly increase the importance of Canada to the requirements of U.S. military security and economic power in the world.

While the U.S. government generally maintains rhetorical support for liberalization of trade throughout the world, when it comes to energy resources the United States is extremely restrictionist. This serves the interests of its domestic producers and ensures American military security. As we shall see the U.S. has no intention of giving up this view of the relation between energy resources and national security. The conclusion of the continental energy deal, therefore, will mean that the U.S. has come to regard our energy resources as extensions of their own domestic supplies. And this can only come about once our government has given its assurance that it will never interfere with the established conditions of U.S. access to our resources. Our energy resources will be admitted freely to the U.S. market only when our government has agreed that it no longer has sovereign power to decide what to do with Canadian resources, and that real sovereignty in deciding a policy for Canadian resources will reside with the U.S. government and American corporations.

As with previous moves to integrate our economy with that of the U.S., the Canadian government will justify the energy deal on the grounds that it will result in great economic benefits to Canadians. The experts will picture continental integration as the only route to jobs and prosperity for the Canadian people. Our government will be exultant that, at long last, it has secured complete access for Canadian energy resources to the world's largest market. Our government will consider no alternative development strategies and its pundits will brush aside the long-term implications of the energy deal.

*   *   *   *   *

In the U.S. acute public concern with energy resources began in the fall of 1969 when the Federal Power Commission produced a report which showed that for the first time in history the use of natural gas began to outstrip the discovery of new reserves. Throughout the fall and winter of 1969-70, the natural gas shortage mounted in the U.S. Columbia Gas System Inc., the largest American gas utility, warned its customers that its demands for the winter of 1970-71 far exceeded the gas it would have. Other major gas companies have turned down new customers in large numbers. Consolidated Edison in New York has refused to build a $370 million power plant addition because it cannot be sure of a supply of gas and because anti-pollution regulations in New York say the plant must use natural gas.[1] One reason for the immense new demand for natural gas is the fact that it is the fuel which pollutes least. In the era of the fight against pollution, natural gas is becoming *the critical resource* for the production of electricity. Its abundance will be a factor of paramount importance in industry in the same way that hydro-electricity has been thus far.

The shortage of natural gas in the U.S. quickly resulted in pressure for long-term commitments by Canada to export great quantities of the fuel to the United States. By the summer of 1970, five applications for the export of natural gas from Canada to the United States were before the National Energy Board in Ottawa. The U.S. thirst for gas was so great that the American Federal Power Commission proceeded on the assumption that a continental energy deal was certain. On July 20, 1970, the FPC approved the building of a $37.2 million gas pipeline from Michigan and Wisconsin to Canada. Incredibly, the Federal Power Commission allowed the natural gas company to proceed before the Canadian National Energy Board had even recommended to the Canadian cabinet the export of the 250 million cubic feet of gas sought daily.[2]

By August, 1970, the Canadian government was close to an agreement to export 9 trillion cubic feet of natural gas worth three

— 3 —

billion dollars to the U.S. over the next 20 to 25 years. Jean Luc Pepin, Minister of Industry, Trade and Commerce, said in Yellowknife on August 10 that a cabinet committee on which he sits would make the final decision within a few weeks. On natural gas, he said:

"It would be crazy to sit on it. In maybe 25 to 50 years we'll be heating ourselves from the rays of the sun and then we'd kick ourselves in the pants for not capitalizing on what we had when gas and oil was a current commodity."[3]

A few days later, when U.S. Secretary of the Interior, Walter Hickel, arrived in Montreal to take off for his tour of the Canadian north, he said he thought it would be good for both countries if a continental energy policy could be agreed upon to cover all forms of energy, even those that had not been discovered yet.[4]

With the Canadian cabinet warning that our energy resources would be useless if we didn't hurry, and with the U.S. cabinet increasing its pressure for a continental energy deal, it appeared that the deal was practically a *fait accompli*. It was to begin with natural gas. In 1970 about half of Canadian natural gas production was already flowing to the United States. The vast amount sought by the Americans threatened to send consumer prices in Canada rocketing. Absurdly it threatened to make it more difficult for Canadian industry to switch to the non-polluting fuel.

The reason that natural gas prices would be driven up in Canada if the gas deal went through is that a free market for gas in North America would cause the Canadian price to move toward the American price – and the American price is rising. U.S. natural gas prices will rise sharply because the Federal Power Commission's policy of holding them down is responsible for the lack of exploration which, in part, explains the current American shortage.[5] James Kerr, chairman of Trans Canada Pipelines Ltd. of Toronto predicted the effects that the export of natural gas would have in Canada:

"While gas producers benefit, the upward pressure on price, combined with the inflationary effects in the cost of expansion, may reach a point where Western Canadian gas may price itself out of certain segments of the Canadian market."[6]

Furthermore the most accessible gas for export is also the most accessible gas for domestic use. This means that we are contemplating exporting the gas that can be brought into production most easily. Because this will deplete our best resources much more quickly, it will force us to depend for future use on more distant and inaccessible sources which will be more expensive to bring into production. Thus we are commiting ourselves to increasing costs in the long as well as in the short run.

A 1969 publication of the National Energy Board in Ottawa made an assessment of U.S. demand for natural gas between now and 1990. It estimated that by 1990 the U.S. would be able to supply itself with only two thirds of its needs from domestic supply. The rest would come from synthetic gas and from imports. It was assumed that by 1990 Canada could be called upon to supply about 8 times as much natural gas to the U.S. annually as it does at present.[7] By then two-thirds of Canadian natural gas would be flowing to the U.S. and this assumes that production in Canada will increase six-fold over the next 20 years. The same publication estimates that over the next 20 years U.S. demand for Canadian oil could increase 11 fold and could constitute well over half of Canadian production.[8] And, of course, the gas and oil industries are virtually the same industry, since the exploration and development of one is the same as for the other.

It is highly significant that a publication of the National Energy Board assumes that the U.S. will be Canada's only possible customer for oil and natural gas over the next 20 years. It reveals something of the way our government uses predictions about future technology to suit its own purposes. The National Energy Board is being very conservative in assuming that technological developments will not make possible large scale exports of natural gas by ocean tanker (at the moment this is not practical); on the other hand, Jean Luc Pepin is expansive in assuming that within a few decades natural gas may well be a horse and buggy fuel in a nirvana of solar energy. In fact, it is obvious that overseas export of natural gas will almost certainly be possible before natural gas loses its usefulness. And yet the government in finding a pseudo-sophisticated argument for its policies, is inclined to reverse these probabilities.

The direction of Canadian government policy is clear. As the National Energy Board Publication points out:

"There has been speculation regarding some form of 'continental energy policy'. Though the phrase may have different meanings for different people, it is frequently taken to mean that Canada and the United States should have a similar policy regarding imports in order to integrate for mutual benefit the development of resources and the crude oil supply pattern of both countries."[9]

The U.S. fears regarding a shortage of natural gas came at the same time as it began to appear that the United States was on the brink of drastic electric power shortages. At the end of 1969, the American Federal Power Commission realized that its previous estimates of U.S. power needs was drastically short. By the summer of 1970, the United States was faced with the prospect of power brown-outs; a long hot spell could mean idle periods for parts of American industry.

The power shortage presented American officials with a number of problems, none of which were easily soluble. One difficulty stemmed from the archaic nature of most of the American power industry, which consists of many firms that are privately owned. Although the U.S. is the world's largest user of electricity, the U.S. does not have a fully integrated and publicly owned power system. This means the system is constantly prone to local and regional failures that would not be a problem in a single vast system. Furthermore, U.S. business and government does not want to solve its power problems through public ownership as Ontario did as early as 1905.

To make matters worse, the U.S. power shortage came at a time when there was immense public pressure against pollution. This meant that the American industry was straining to expand in the face of vocal pressure groups that were fighting new projects that would be detrimental to the environment.

All this pointed to the desirability of an electric power grid that is continent-wide, in which power from Canada would be available during peak load periods for industrialized sections of the U.S. Involvement in such arrangements again raised the crucial need to define the Canadian interest. And selling electricity to the U.S. was one field in which Canadians had already had their fingers severely burned. During World War II, when Canada was desperately attempting to gear up for wartime production, the U.S. refused to allow Canada to take back power for its own use that it had been exporting to the U.S. on a yearly basis.[10]

During the winter of 1970, events moved quickly on the energy front. At the end of February, a U.S. cabinet task force on oil imports, issued the Shultz Report. The report favoured replacing U.S. import quotas on crude oil with tariffs. The Shultz report concluded that it was in the interest of American national security to achieve a fully harmonized energy resource policy with Canada. Chapter three deals with the Shultz Report extensively.

A month after the Shultz Report was issued, the U.S. imposed a quota on Canadian crude oil imports, cutting them back to 395,000 barrels a day. Two months later a White House letter to a U.S. Senator explained that the quota was aimed at pressuring Canada into a long term energy arrangement.[11] In the space of a few months, the energy shortage had become a matter of acute public concern in the United States; the U.S. had articulated its need for an energy deal with Canada; and with the oil quota, the arm twisting had begun to force Canada into the energy deal.

These events in the U.S. brought J. J. Greene, Canada's Minister of Energy, Mines and Resources to centre-stage in the continental energy game. One week a continentalist, the next week a supposed nationalist, Greene contrived to surround the discussions of energy resources with a cloud of confusion. When he returned from his conference with U.S. Interior Secretary Walter Hickel in December, 1969, he was full of scorn for what he called "narrow nationalism". His head spun with the excitement of a continental energy deal. The angry response to the proposed continental deal from many quarters in Canada, and subsequent events in the U.S., revealed to Greene that he was in danger of ending up cast in the role of villain in another 1956 style pipeline debate. But J. J. Greene is nothing if not a sensitive politician. He quickly changed the script.

In May, 1970, he delivered his famous address to the Independent Petroleum Association of America, in Denver, Colorado. Apparently through with continentalism, Greene sounded like a Quebec premier at a federal-provincial conference — full of heady phrases about his people back home, but ready to be reasonable on bread and butter matters once the emotional air had been cleared.

In their reports Canadian newspapers mainly seized on the sensational postures that Greene struck at Denver. They picked up his stated disillusionment with the American dream, in the era of Vietnam, campus disorder, and black disaffection.[12] They were titillated by his hint that some day Canada might consider jamming the air waves to keep out American television programming.[13] They detailed his moving rendition of the sorrows Canadians feel because the National Hockey League has been alienated into American hands.[14] These things were all very well, of course, but they had nothing to do with Greene's Department of Energy, Mines and Resources.

In his speech, Greene made a number of substantive comments on matters bearing on resources policy and it is important to keep in mind just what those points were. First, he made the point that the Canadian government found it difficult to negotiate with the U.S. on energy matters while under the gun of the U.S. quota of 395,000 barrels a day for Canadian crude oil imposed in March, 1970. He pointed here to the political difficulty created by the U.S. quota in the minds of the folks back home:

"The unilateral action on quotas has created for us grave political problems which I am very sure were not considered by U.S. officials who recommended the arbitrary shut-off and restrictions. Canadian public opinion is interpreting this as a pressure play, to squeeze Canada into some form of energy deal which would not be to the Canadian advantage."[15]

He then said that what Canada wanted were "realistic trading arrangements in respect of oil which would secure that Canadian oil enters United States markets on a normal commercial basis."

"I recognize that this simple goal may prove difficult of attainment. But I am confident as to ultimate success because I believe that such an outcome would be entirely consistent with the basic complementarity of resources and requirements in the two countries and the mutual benefit of our two peoples."[16]

Greene's next point referred to the touchy matter of the security of Canadian oil. Here he showed indignation at the idea that in the event that an international crisis cut off overseas oil from the eastern Canadian market, Canada might ship Alberta oil to eastern Canada and forget about the areas in the United States that had become dependent on Canadian oil. Canada would not renege on its agreements, he said.[17]

He then told his audience that the Canadian National Energy Board was at that moment reviewing its criteria for deciding how much Canadian natural gas could be regarded as surplus and made available for export.[18] Here he made his tough point:

". . . Canadian gas will be available to supplement United States supplies only if our petroleum industry as a whole receives the incentives of progressive growth and assured stability of access to export markets for oil and natural gas liquids."[19]

In other words the government was willing to be tougher about natural gas in order to open up the U.S. market for Canadian oil.

Continuing with a swipe at the Canadian government's much maligned White Paper on Taxation, Greene said that it was unlikely that in implementing tax reform the government would ride roughshod over the petroleum industry's best interests.

"In particular, I cannot see that it would legislate a tax climate in which the Canadian petroleum industry would be put at any significantly increased disadvantage compared with the industry in the U.S.", he said.[20]

This could only be taken to mean that the Canadian petroleum industry would continue to enjoy the light tax load with depletion allowances and loopholes that has always been its happy lot in the U.S.

Finally on the issue of foreign ownership of Canadian resources, Greene said that Canadians were determined that "a substantial proportion of the future growth remains in Canadian hands".

He went on to say:

". . . there is no question but that we shall require continuing and increasing sources of investment capital from abroad, if we are to maintain a satisfactory rate of economic growth. We are convinced that this can be accomplished by rules which will achieve a greater and growing proportion of Canadian ownership and still provide a just return to the foreign investor."[21]

Greene did not explain how more foreign investment and greater Canadian ownership would be achieved, so that his remarks remained reminiscent of politicians who promise to lower taxes, spend more and balance the budget.

Greene's Denver speech, when looked at point by point, is continentalist to the core. What he is saying is that Canada is available and secure as a source of energy resources and as a site for continued foreign investment; and to top it all off, bargain basement tax rates are guaranteed to continue in the resource field. In return, Greene is asking for less heavy handedness on the part of the U.S. in its negotiations and a greater share of the continental pie for Canadian big business.

Greene's Denver speech faces up to none of the important questions that should be asked when talking about energy exports to the U.S. He does not challenge the present ownership pattern of the Canadian petroleum industry; he does not point to establishing a tax rate on petroleum that would bring it into line with the tax payments of other industries; and he does not raise the question of refining crude oil in Canada before exporting it to the U.S.

It is hard to imagine why the Denver oilmen should have been concerned with the speech, unless of course the cultural peculiarities Greene ascribed to himself and his fellow Canadians were too much for their zenophobia. But in the end, American oilmen will undoubtedly agree that provided they get what they want from Canada economically, Canadians can indulge in whatever cultural oddities they desire.

In the period from December, 1969 to May, 1970, then, despite all the media talk of conversion, Greene had merely switched his rhetoric while remaining fundamentally a continentalist.

As Greene moved from event to event through the winter months of 1970, he had the appearance of a fleeting figure in Canadian politics. There were rumours that he might be out of the cabinet by the time the serious bargaining began. Greene in no way had shaped the context for the discussion on energy. In fact, the model for a possible energy deal between Canada and the United States had been outlined most clearly, in terms of the principles involved, half a decade before, in the Merchant-Heeney Report of 1965. The Merchant-Heeney report was produced by the U.S. ambassador to Canada and the Canadian ambassador to Washington, following discussions between Prime Minister Pearson and President Johnson in the U.S. capital in January 1964. The Prime Minister and the President charged Merchant and Heeney "with the task of examining the desirability and practicability of developing acceptable principles which would make it easier to avoid divergencies in economic and other policies of interest to each other."[22]

The feature of the Merchant-Heeney Report at the time of its publication that received the most comment was the recommendation that Canada restrict itself to quiet diplomacy in its relations with the United States, avoiding public disagreement as much as possible. The report stated that "It is important and reasonable that Canadian authorities should have careful regard for the United States Government's position in . . . (the) . . . world context, and, in the absence of special Canadian interests and obligations, avoid so far as possible, public disagreement especially upon critical issues."[23]

Behind this conclusion in the report was a whole rationale for the way in which the Canadian and American governments should deal with each other. In general, Merchant and Heeney called for what could be called a functionalist approach to Canadian-American relations which would feature important questions more as technical matters than as political questions. The report called for the following general method of procedure:

"In certain fields where combined efforts are called for, such as continental air defence arrangements and joint development of resources, there is obvious advantage in having the consultative process begin at the planning stage so as to facilitate concurrent formulation of policy."[24]

The report was explicit about the need to move toward a continental approach to the development of energy resources, particularly in the case of electrical energy. The report referred to "the economic advantages to both countries of disregarding the boundary for energy purposes, that is, in the development and distribution of energy on a regional north-south basis where this is to the mutual advantage." The report did not limit itself to a discussion of electrical energy alone but concluded that "we believe there would be virtue in having a joint look at the energy picture as a whole."[25]

The current approach to talks on energy resources appears to bear much similarity to the blueprint set out in the Merchant-Heeney Report. There is a clear disposition to think in regional north-south terms rather than in national terms.

One enthusiast for the principles of resource sharing on a north-south basis, was the newly appointed deputy minister of energy, Mines and Resources, Jack Austin. For him the model to emulate was the Columbia River Treaty, whose example had already inspired Merchant and Heeney in their Report.[26] In a speech before the Bar Association in the year before his appointment, Austin said:

"While no general principles may have been established in law as a result of its language, certainly we hope that the practice of resource sharing as explained in the Columbia River Treaty is an indication of the tendency of the same parties to deal with other resource problems in the same way."[27]

Austin's appointment by Prime Minister Trudeau was seen as a new experiment in bringing businessmen into public service. When Trudeau appointed the 34 year old mining promoter from Vancouver he underlined the fact that the appointment "reflects the government's desire to encourage leading men in industry and business to enter the government service."[28]

In a recent article, Professor Vaughan Lyon of Trent University raised a number of serious questions about Austin's appointment:

"Mr. Austin comes to this sensitive top policy making position from a short but highly successful career in promoting a number of mining ventures in Vancouver and an even briefer period in Government service before that. His appointment resembles those in

U.S. Government in several ways. He comes from one of the industries for which he is now expected to recommend policy.

"The announcement of his appointment states that he has severed his connections in the private sector '. . . during such time as he remains in the Government service'. Clearly, Mr. Austin is free, without moral or legal restriction, to resume his association with the mining industry after he leaves government service, and to work under the policies which he has helped to establish. The release also suggests that Mr. Austin's tenure in office is not expected to be a long one, but it will coincide with negotiations with Washington which could affect the interests of Canadian firms and interests for a generation."[29]

Perhaps Austin, and not Greene, will prove to be the key figure in negotiating the continental energy deal. In any case, whatever the situation in the rather confused Department of Energy, Mines and Resources, there are governmental and corporate forces on this continent that are moving with a sense of sureness toward a final solution for Canadian resources.

On July 9, 1970 a Globe and Mail profile introduced the new president of Imperial Oil Ltd. to the Canadian people. J. A. Armstrong, a native of Dauphin, Manitoba, was said to be possessed of the confident, yet restrained corporate image that befits the president of a subsidiary of Standard Oil of New Jersey. Imperial presides over the greatest reserves of any oil company in Canada. Armstrong said his company favours the idea of pooling North American energy sources in a continental policy. He feels certain that the United States will need increasing quantities of Canadian oil, but that a Canadian commitment to a continental approach is needed so that the industry can begin to formulate long-term planning.

It appears that Armstrong is unimpressed with the frenetic twists and turns in Joe Greene's office. He stated that Imperial is already proceeding with its exploration programme in the belief that the two governments will eventually harmonize their policies on resource development and use.[30] Armstrong's views on continental energy policy are typical of Canadian as well as of U.S. businessmen. On February 3, 1970 Robert Fowler, co-chairman of the influential Canadian-American Committee and president of the Canadian Pulp and Paper Association, told the House of Commons Committee on External Affairs and National Defence that "the greater danger is not American aggression but American neglect."[31]

Oilmen in the United States are equally confident that a continental energy approach is just around the corner. "Petroleum Today" is the publication of the American Petroleum Institute. It is a publication that reflects the "middle American" values of Spiro Agnew that are so congenial to oilmen.

"Petroleum Today" sang the praises of the great adventure of the Manhattan as it sailed through the North-West passage in the summer of 1969. The publication did not bother to mention that the Manhattan was sailing through Canadian waters.[32] Another article in the magazine, after discussing the possibility of shipping Alaska oil by sea, made the following statement:

"A more breath-taking scheme would be to run the pipeline up along the Mackenzie River and across Western Canada to Edmonton. There it would hook into the Interprovincial Pipeline, which has its terminus in Chicago. The pipeline would be 3,300 hundred miles long: the longest one in the Free World."[33]

In case anyone hopes that no major changes in Canada's export pattern of energy resources can take place without a full debate in parliament, he should look at the National Energy Board Act of 1959. The Act authorized extension of export and import provisions regarding oil by order in council. An amendment to the Act in 1966 increased the quantities of electric power and other energy that the board may authorize for export through cabinet order.[34]

The energy crisis creates a fundamental problem for Canadians. It is not easy to determine the resource needs of a country. It depends on the criteria one uses. The Liberals, although they have been neglectful and incompetent, even in applying their own criteria, do have a set of assumptions which they use to decide the resource needs of Canada. They make two central assumptions: first, that Canada will always be, relatively speaking, a hinterland of the United States; and secondly, that the short run desire for profit is and should remain the key determinant of the allocation of resources. Even if the Liberals had done their work properly and had designed a national resources policy based on these two assumptions, it would have meant disaster for Canada. The first assumption means accepting colonialism as a permanent status for Canada; the second assumption means the destruction of the natural environment of this and any other country where this policy is continued. To make a long run commitment to export Canadian resources to the United States based on these criteria is criminal at a time when Canadians are expressing an increased desire for independence and when people all over the world are coming to realize that we cannot continue to despoil our environment as we have.

II RESOURCES IN THE CANADIAN POLITICAL ECONOMY

It is important to understand the centrality of Canadian resources to Canadian society as a whole. One can state without exaggeration that Canadian resources have always played a key role in determining Canada's relations with the outside world. To a peculiar degree, Canada has always been dependent on the export of one or a few staple products. The desire for Canadian staple products preceded and was responsible for the peopling of the country itself. From the cod fisheries, through furs, timber and wheat to minerals, Canada has served as a resource hinterland to a more developed and industrialized society. In the 19th century, Canadian staples flowed to Britain; today they flow south to the United States. In the days when our staple trade gave a material basis to our links with Britain, Canadian independence in North America was assisted by our dependent place within an empire based across the sea. Our role today as resource hinterland to the world's most powerful state, our next door neighbour, threatens us with a transition that is not to independence, but rather to political and social disintegration. The "old" staples — fish, furs, timber and wheat — created an east-west axis for Canadian commerce. Thus dependency on a metropolis across the sea carried with it the promise of national economic development for Canada and eventual independence. The "new" staples — nickel, iron ore, oil, natural gas — have been exported from north to south, thus contributing to the economic and political balkanization of Canada.

Concentration on resource exports has always meant colonialism for Canada. In his classic study, *The Fur Trade in Canada*, Harold Innis draws the following conclusions about the effects of the staples on Canadian economy and society:

"The economic history of Canada has been dominated by the discrepancy between the centre and the margin of western civilization. Energy has been directed toward the exploitation of staple products and the tendency has been cumulative. The raw material supplied to the mother country stimulated manufacturers of the finished product and also of the products which were in demand in the colony. Large-scale production of raw materials was encouraged by improvement of technique of production, of marketing, and of transport, as well as by improvement in the manufacture of the finished product. As a consequence, energy in the colony was drawn into the production of the staple commodity both directly and indirectly. Population was involved directly in the production of the staple and indirectly in the production of facilities promoting production. Agriculture, industry, transportation, trade, finance, and governmental activities tend to become subordinate to the production of the staple for a more highly specialized manufacturing community."[1]

We have always been a subordinate people, a derivative people, because of our origin and our history as resource exporters. Our staple products have been the real chains of empire that have bound us first to Britain and now to the United States. It is through our resources that we have related most profoundly to mankind as a whole.

Herman Kahn once described Canada as "a regional power without a region". His unkind quip lays bare the reality that has created so many neuroses for people around the External Affairs Department who have wanted to keep alive for Canada the role of a "middle power". As the American presence in Canada has grown and as the Commonwealth has declined, it has become obvious to almost everyone that Canada has become a political dependency of the United States. Securely within the American Empire, economically and politically, Canadian business has itself engaged in imperial ventures in the Caribbean and Latin America. But it is clear that in terms of international diplomacy, we don't amount to much. Within the narrow spectrum of establishment politics, our foreign policy has turned on moral gestures, which usually consist of minor criticism of the Americans within a context of almost total support for their policies in the world.

The truth is that while no one pays much attention to the presence of Canadian diplomacy, the presence of Canadian resources are a factor of real importance in the world political arena. Our involvement in the Vietnam war has much more to do with the metals and the guns we sell to the United States than with our

– 16 –

presence on the International Control Commission. Canadian oil, as a substitute for middle eastern oil for the United States and her allies, is potentially a far more important factor in the options open to the great powers in the middle east than any peacekeeping force we may ever have imagined.

Obviously if Canadian resources are a factor of importance in world politics, their disposition will be absolutely vital in determining the economic and political future of the Canadian people.

Many Canadians look forward to a situation in which we will be able to sell more energy resources to the U.S., believing that this will result in greater well-being for this country. In fact, for a variety of reasons an energy deal with the U.S. will lead to economic underdevelopment for Canada. It will heighten the problem of unemployment in the Canadian economy and it will mean the final demise of Canadian sovereignty in basic economic questions.

The first thing that has to be remembered is the overwhelming extent of U.S. ownership of Canadian resource industries. Trade Minister Jean Luc Pepin recently revealed these percentages of foreign ownership to the House of Commons: 99.9 per cent of oil refining; 82.6 per cent of the oil and gas wells industry; and 84.9 per cent of primary metal smelting and refining. The key components of the Canadian resource sector are dominated by huge vertically-integrated American conglomerates. These firms, many of which are involved in all levels of production from mineral extraction to final manufacturing, are able to set "world" prices which are advantageous to them.

⌐ It has been characteristic of the capitalist international economy since World War II that the prices of raw materials have risen much less sharply than have the prices of manufactured goods. What this means is that the terms of trade for resource extracting countries has been worsening for at least the past quarter century⌟ Dominion Bureau of Statistics figures reveal the trends for Canada. The price index for crude raw materials exported from Canada in 1968 stood at 140.4 compared to the standard 100 for 1948; the prices of end products exported from Canada stood at 174.4 in 1968 compared to the 1948 standard of 100. The figures for imports are equally striking. Crude raw material imports stood at 110.8 in 1968, while end product imports stood at 164.7 in terms of the standard 100 for 1948.[2] Over the past twenty years, the trend in Canadian exports has been away from crude raw materials toward fabricated materials and end products. However, by 1968 only 35 per cent of Canadian exports were end products compared with 61 per cent of our imports.[3]

Furthermore, the price of crude oil (the key price in any energy deal) has been dropping on a world-wide basis for some time. This results from the existence of a relative oil surplus in the world which it is estimated will last until at least 1980.[4] It also results from the fact that the price-fixing arrangements of the major oil companies have begun to break down in the face of competition from the so-called "independents" among oil companies, thus resulting in a decline from the previously artificially high price of crude oil.

There is at present a vast disparity in price between American oil and middle eastern and Venezuelan oil. The U.S. market has been protected for high cost domestic producers. As the Shultz Report states:

"In 1969, consumers paid about $5 billion more for oil products than they would have paid in the absence of import restrictions."[5]

The present wellhead price of Middle Eastern crude oil is $1.40 per barrel compared with $3.30 per barrel for South Louisiana crude[6] and $2.60 at Edmonton.

An energy resources deal with the United States would sharply reverse the trend in our exports which has been away from raw materials. If the projections of the National Energy Board are correct, the bulk of a vastly increased supply of Canadian oil and natural gas will flow south over the next 20 years.

A greatly increased output of oil and natural gas in Canada can only result from tremendous investments in exploration and development. These investments will come either directly from the U.S. or from the profits of U.S. subsidiaries in Canada. The new investment will not be channeled into diversifying the Canadian economy, but into deepening our dependence on the resource sector. As a necessary result of this immense investment in developing the resource sector, Canadians will be forced to buy more and more U.S. manufactured goods. Over the long haul we will be committing ourselves to purchasing goods whose prices are rising more rapidly than the prices of the goods we sell. We will be forced to sell more and more raw materials to buy back the same quantity of manufactured goods. It is just this process that has led to the impoverishment of Latin America. In relative terms, Canada would be on the way to the economic status of a banana republic.

That the U.S. is banking on the propensity of American owned firms in Canada to send profits home and to generate purchases from the U.S. is clear. The Shultz Report, in considering the import of much more Canadian oil, assumes that 71 per cent of the dollars which U.S. companies brought into Canada to finance their expanded capacity would return to the United States in the same year in the form of profits or purchases.[7]

This form of exploitation of our raw materials will not lead to the processing of our resources in Canada. We will not proceed toward the establishment of a petro-chemical industry in this way; nor will we even refine the greatly increased quantities of Canadian oil that are destined for the U.S. market. We will not refine our oil in Canada for export or process our raw materials here because it is not in the interest of U.S. corporations to undertake those activities here. And the U.S. will only enter into the energy deal on terms which it regards as in its self-interest.

This increased dependence of Canadians on raw materials, at the expense of manufacturing, would mean that we would suffer from a permanently acute rate of unemployment. Resource industries are heavily capital intensive; they employ few people. In 1968 the mining sector of the Canadian economy paid out 878.3 million dollars in wages and salaries, while the manufacturing sector paid out 9,143.9 million dollars. Resource industries are immense profit makers for their foreign owners but they provide few jobs. It is no accident that unemployment is typically higher in the extractive Canadian economy than in the more industrialized U.S. economy; an energy deal would heighten this tendency in future.

Furthermore, the mining industry in Canada has been getting away with highway robbery when it comes to paying taxes. In 1965 while profits in mining totalled 602 million dollars, taxable income came to only 162.6 million dollars.[8] Thus, while mining produced 12 per cent of total Canadian corporate profits in 1965, its share of taxable profits came to only 4 per cent of the total. Again in 1967, while the book profit of the mining industry came to over 736 million dollars, the taxable income of the industry was rated at only 184 million dollars once all the tax loopholes had been figured in.[9]

Finally, there is the much publicized myth that multi-national corporations provide countries like Canada with much needed foreign investment. The reality is that large foreign corporations are designed for taking surplus, in the form of profits, out of a country in which they operate for the benefit of shareholders at home. Over three quarters of so-called new American investment in Canada comes in the form of the reinvestment of profits earned in Canada. And, as Cy Gonick points out, between 1960 and 1967 "Canadian subsidiaries and affiliates sent $1 billion more to their parent companies in the form of profits ($2 billion more if royalties, licence and management fees were included) than they received from them in the form of capital imports."[10]

It may be useful for us to examine briefly the behaviour of the ultimate multi-national corporation, Standard Oil of New Jersey. In 1962 Jersey Standard controlled 198 subsidiaries outside the United States, including 37 in Canada through its 69.8 per cent ownership of Imperial Oil. The assets of Jersey Standard approached eleven and a half billion dollars and its profit was 841 million dollars. In their book, *Monopoly Capital,* Baron and Sweezy comment on Jersey Standard's investment policies abroad:

"The tremendous variety and scope of Jersey's foreign operations might lead one to suppose that over the years the company has been a large and consistent exporter of capital. Nothing could be further from the truth. Apart from a small initial export of capital many years ago, the expansion of Jersey's foreign assets has been financed from the profits of its foreign operations. Moreover, so great have been these foreign profits that after all foreign expansion needs have been taken care of, there have still been huge sums left over for remittance to the parent company in the United States. . . . In that year (1962) as already noted, total profits were $841 million. Of this sum, $538 million were paid out as dividends to stockholders, the vast majority of whom are residents of the United States. The remaining $303 million were added to the company's investments, at home and abroad. Elsewhere in the same Annual Report that records these figures, we learn that profits from operations in the United States in 1962 were $309 million. This figure, it will be seen, is $229 million less than the amount of dividends paid. In other words, approximately 40 per cent of dividends paid to stockholders, plus whatever net investment was made in the United States during the year, were financed from the profits of foreign operations. In a word: Standard Oil of New Jersey is a very large and consistent *importer* of capital."[11]

In 1969 Jersey Standard's Canadian subsidiary, Imperial Oil, had the highest sales of any public corporation in Canada and made a profit of 94 million dollars.[12]

Typically, people think of a company like Imperial Oil simply as a large company in the oil business. The truth is that Imperial is like a feudal fiefdom. It is held from above by the majestic giant of all multi-national corporations, Jersey Standard. But below it are its own subsidiaries. Imperial is typical of the large resource complexes in Canada. To give an idea of what such a complex looks like, here are the holdings of Imperial Oil as of 1965, according to DBS figures. The percentage indicates the extent of Imperial's ownership of the company:

1. Carnduff Gas Ltd. 25.1%
2. Montreal Pipe Line Co. Ltd. 32.0%
3. Tecumseh Gas Storage Ltd. 50.0%
4. Smiley Gas Conservation Ltd. 47.0%
5. Syndcrude (Canada) Ltd. 30.0%
6. Alberta Gas Trunk Line Co. Ltd. 10.7%
7. Redwater Water Disposal Co. Ltd. 44.7%
8. Nottingham Gas Ltd. 35.3%
9. Mitsue Pipe Line Ltd. 33.3%
10. Atlas Supply Co. (Canada) Ltd. 100.0%
11. Bourque Bros. Ltd. 90%
12. Building Products (Canada) Ltd. 100%
13. Champlain Oil Products Ltd. .100.0%
14. Devon Estates Ltd. 100.0%
15. Devonian Natural Gas Co. Ltd. 99.9%
16. Home Oil Distributors Ltd. 100.0%
17. Imperial Oil Developments Ltd. 99.9%
18. Imperial Oil Enterprises Ltd. .100.0%
19. Imperial Pipe Line Co. Ltd. 100.0%
20. Interprovincial Pipe Line Co. .33.0%
21. Maple Leaf Petroleum Ltd. 99.4%
22. Mongeau and Robert Cie Ltd. .99.8%
23. Murphy J. Fuel Oil Co. Ltd. .100.0%
24. Nisku Products Pipe Line Co. Ltd. 99.4%
25. Oval Natural Gas Co. Ltd. 99.8%
26. Paley Bottle Ltd. 100.0%
27. Seaway Bunkers Ltd. 16.7%
28. Servacar Ltd. 70.0%
29. St. Lawrence Tankers Ltd. 50%
30. Winnipeg Pipe Line Co. Ltd. .100.0%

30214

To broaden and deepen the power of companies like Jersey Standard in Canada is to ensure that larger and larger amounts of surplus will flow out of this country to the United States. While the energy deal will provide jobs to put in the infrastructure of pipelines, tankers, etc. for a continental energy system, this period of employment will be of temporary duration and of limited scope. Once the system is fully operative, Canada will have lost the comparative advantage of having at its disposal accessible resources in abundance upon which to base economic development and diversification in this country. The energy resources deal will give the Americans equal access to these resources. Given their comparative advantage in industry and given the almost total integration of the two economies which has resulted from past policies and which will occur even more following the energy deal it becomes clear that Canada would never overcome its position as a hinterland.

The danger of the energy deal is not that Canada will face an absolute shortage of either natural gas or oil, but that we will be moving into a state of greater economic dependency on the U.S. The energy deal will make the Canadian economy more of a hinterland economy. Growth in much of Canada will be based even more on the expansion of raw materials exports and not on economic diversification. One important result of economic dependency is that it increases the inability of the hinterland country ever to become technologically advanced. In an Article in Canadian Forum, Kari Levitt points to "the relative decline in local entrepreneurship in contemporary English-speaking Canada as compared with the late nineteenth and early twentieth century".

She states:

"A branch-plant economy dependent on imported technology is assured of a perpetual technological backwardness vis-a-vis the metropolis. Furthermore, dependence is addictive and the dynamics of dependence are cumulative."[14]

Having witnessed the decline of the aircraft industry in Canada and now the unlikelihood of a Canadian future in the electronics industry and the extremely low level of research and development work in general in the Canadian economy, we can see how dependency erodes the possibility of running one's own economy.

Some might argue that we can move in the direction of becoming a much greater exporter of raw materials to the U.S. with U.S. companies controlling the resource industries and at the same time diversify our economy. But the evidence is all the other way. The plain fact is that the Canadian business class that has been running the Canadian economy for the past hundred years has not been able to promote any thing like balanced and diversified economic development. To date, only the Toronto and Montreal areas have been industrialized in a major way. Most of the rest of Canada is either stagnant economically or dependent on a very narrow economic base of raw materials extraction.

The key point is that the energy deal means much more of the same. In fact, it means such a major new commitment to the continuance of a hinterland economy that economic diversification and greater relative industrialization becomes virtually impossible.

III U.S. RESOURCE NEEDS AND
CANADA SINCE WORLD WAR II

The U.S. assault on Canadian resources has been building up for over a century. From the time of the lumber trade of the 1850's which devastated the forests in much of what is now Ontario, American businesses have revealed a growing interest in Canadian resources. Following World War I, the growth of the pulp and paper industry and the opening of the mineral areas of northern Ontario and Quebec greatly tightened the ties between American investors and Canadian resources.

By the end of World War II, the United States had become the predominant world power; Britain had lost its imperial stature; and Canada had moved definitively from the British Empire through a brief period of independence into the American Empire. U.S. direct investment in Canada and Canadian membership in the U.S. military alliance system became the main features of the post-war world for Canadians.

With world power came a growing U.S. dependence on raw materials from many countries. Throughout the 20th century, the U.S. had gradually shifted from the position of an exporter to an importer of raw materials. By 1956-60 the United States was importing over half of all its required metals.[1] Even earlier, the Korean war had made the Americans acutely aware of their strategic reliance on resources from many countries.

The need for access to resources was presented to the American people as a part of the world-wide anti-communist crusade. In June, 1952, the report of President Truman's Materials Policy Commission was published with the title *Resources for Freedom*. Known as the Paley report, the study advocated a systematic attempt on the part of the U.S. to gain access to the resources of its allies and satellites, the world over. U.S. investment in resource rich countries would be followed by the dependence of those countries on U.S.

manufacturing — all to the benefit of American business and American security. The Paley Report summed up U.S. objectives as follows:

"The over-all objective of a national Materials Policy for the United States should be to insure an adequate and dependable flow of materials at the lowest cost consistent with national security and with the welfare of friendly nations."[2]

The Paley Report simply rationalized a U.S. resource grab policy that was far advanced. By the time of the Paley Report, U.S. direct investment in Canada had reached mammoth proportions. Since then, U.S. corporations have gained predominance in the key manufacturing, and resource sectors of the Canadian economy.

By the end of the 1960's the U.S. had come to depend on Canada not only for immense profits, but also for strategic supplies in maintaining the military power on which the Americans depended for their control of much of the globe. One corporation alone, International Nickel (INCO) supplied the U.S. with the bulk of its vital nickel as well as sending its investors, a majority of whom are American, a net profit of one hundred and forty-three and a half million dollars in 1968. Aluminum, copper, and zinc, as well as nickel and other metals, flowed from Canada to the U.S.

As the 1960's came to an end, the focus of U.S. interest in Canada became greatly heightened due to the new alarm regarding American supplies of energy resources. A two-fold process was at work: U.S. domestic supplies of natural gas and water-power began to run short; and at the same time the U.S. was becoming increasingly alarmed at the insecurity of its investments in such areas as the Middle East and Latin America. As the American Empire was experiencing crises in many parts of the world, its corporate and military men began to think in deadly earnest about resources in safer areas. An article in *Fortune* Magazine in August 1969 explained the new situation from the point of view of the investor:

"The major risks to today's mining companies are likely to come from the movement of great political forces. When large powers had their way with their colonies, there were few nationalizations or expropriations. Today even small countries, spurred by a growing sense of autonomy and nationalism, are demanding either a greater share of the profits from foreign mining operations, or outright ownership of them . . . A not surprising consequence is that mining firms are poking around more assiduously these days in the "stable" countries."[3]

Canada is indeed a stable country. Governed by a political party that has sought continental integration since the 1880's, Canada has fewer controls on foreign investors than any other major country on earth. Furthermore, Canada is rich in the energy resources, oil, natural gas, water, that the U.S. is becoming concerned about.

As 606 Canadian corporations were taken over from abroad mostly by Americans between 1963 and 1969,[4] the U.S. stake in Canada continued to increase. Takeovers and dreams of future takeovers began by the end of the decade to make the U.S. military aware of the heightened strategic importance of Canada. An article in a U.S. army publication, *Military Review,* stated:

"If the mining potential of the Far North should be tapped, if harbour facilities and storage areas should be constructed, and if giant vessels regularly ply the Northwest passage, then the northern region would suddenly become rich in military targets . . . The U.S. defence posture — for the first time in history — would have to become northern oriented."

When we discuss an energy resources deal between Canada and the United States, it is important to realize that the Americans have been moving toward a continental oil policy for 15 years. In 1954, U.S. president Eisenhower established a cabinet level Advisory Committee on Energy Supplies and Resources Policy to study the security implications of the growing importation of crude oil into the United States from abroad.[5] Growing U.S. imports in crude oil stemmed from the increased competition between the "independents" and the "majors" in the oil industry. Following the report of the Committee which warned that increased imports of crude oil would constitute a threat to U.S. national security, Eisenhower instituted a system of voluntary controls on the importation of crude oil into the United States. In October 1955, the U.S. Office of Defense Mobilization (ODM) exempted Canada and Venezuela from the controls. Arthur S. Flemming, director of ODM, explained this move later when he stated that "it has always been the policy in Government . . . to consider those countries (Venezuela and Canada) and others in this hemisphere as within the U.S. orbit when dealing with defense questions."[6]

A second Eisenhower voluntary import control program removed the exemption on Venezuelan and Canadian crude oil. But this reversal of American policy was soon undone when in 1959 the Eisenhower administration brought in a mandatory program of controls on the importation of crude oil into the United States. On

April 30, 1959 the mandatory program was amended by the exemption of "crude oil, unfinished oils, or finished products which are transported into the United States by pipeline, rail, or other means of overland transportation from the country where they were produced, which country, in the case of unfinished oils or finished products, is also the country of production of the crude oil from which they were processed or manufactured."[7]

This exemption which applied only to Canada was maintained under Eisenhower, Kennedy and Johnson. Under the mandatory program, the import of Canadian crude oil shot ahead while imports from the two other major sources, Venezuela and the Middle East, dropped. In 1959 Canadian crude had accounted for only 8.3 per cent of U.S. imports with Venezuela at 51 per cent and the Middle East at 30.1 per cent. By 1967 the figures were: Canada, 30.2 per cent; Venezuela, 39.6 per cent; and the Middle East 13.7 per cent. (The Canadian figure was higher and the Middle East figure lower due to the Arab-Israeli war of 1967, but it simply advanced the trend.)[8]

In a book on the U.S. oil import program, Edward H. Shaffer concludes that an important reason for Canada's exemption under the program stemmed from a Canadian government threat to build an Alberta to Montreal oil pipeline which would have meant the loss of business to the U.S. companies operating out of Venezuela which were then violently opposed to such a pipeline.[9] But there can be little doubt that Canada's acceptability as a security risk was an important factor. In contrast with Canada, Venezuela got less and less of the U.S. import market under the mandatory program, mainly because the Venezuelan government tried to obtain more of a share of the oil revenues in taxation. For this Venezuela was consciously punished by the U.S. In 1957, the last year that the Venezuelan government accepted bids for new concessions to U.S. oil companies, the capital investment of U.S. oil companies in development in Venezuela totalled $849 million. This dropped to $390 million the next year; by 1966 the figure had declined to $101 million.[10]

Canadian reliability as a source of crude oil was underlined most dramatically during the Middle East crises of 1956 and 1967. Canadian exports of crude oil to the U.S. experienced their greatest gains following these crises. Following the 1967 crisis, the U.S. government agreed to allow the doubling of the capacity of the pipeline connecting the Alberta fields to Billings, Montana, and to permit the Interprovincial line to double its capacity and to go directly into the Chicago area.[11]

The 1967 crisis revealed the severe weakness of the eastern North American oil market to vulnerability in international supply. At present both the North East of the United States and Canada from the Ottawa valley east are dependent on oil imports from the Middle East and Venezuela. It is now clear that the Americans regard eastern Canada as part of their security responsibility.

Canada's exemption under the U.S. program of mandatory crude oil import controls did not mean complete access for Canadian crude to the U.S. market, for a number of reasons. First, there was a definite limit imposed by pipeline and transporation capability in moving Canadian oil to the U.S. Second, the U.S. import system meant that U.S. producers were granted an import quota depending on the amount of domestic crude they used. The use of Canadian crude did not gain them further import points to allow them to purchase cheaper Middle Eastern and Venezuelan oil. Finally in 1967, a Canada-U.S. gentleman's agreement not to flood the U.S. market with cheaper Canadian oil was a factor. However, the quotas on the voluntary agreement were consistently exceeded. By the beginning of 1970, Canadian exports of crude were running as high as 800,000 barrels a day in January and February.

Then came the Shultz report in February, 1970. Entitled, *The Oil Import Question: A Report on the Relationship of Oil Imports to the National Security,* the report was presented by the Cabinet Task Force on Oil Import Control which was appointed by president Nixon shortly after his administration took office. (P. 1 Shultz). The task force, chaired by Secretary of Labor, George P. Shultz, was made up of six cabinet members and personnel from a number of American government bureaus. The task force did not achieve a consensus on the matters under its purview. Three of its members, Secretary of the Interior, Walter Hickel, Secretary of Commerce, Maurice H. Stans, and Chairman of the Federal Power Commission, John N. Nassikas submitted a separate report.

The central issue in contention between the main and the separate report was whether the U.S. should move to a tariff for the import of crude oil (the majority position) or retain its import quota system on a modified basis (the minority position). Both groups within the task force were agreed on the great importance of dependable oil supply to American national security. They were disagreed on the degree of the security problem and on how to protect national security (through tariffs or quotas). The separate report came down harder on the side of restrictiveness for the sake of security, or for the sake of the domestic oil lobby depending on your interpretation.

The main report sets out the kinds of security problems to be considered in arriving at a U.S. oil policy as follows:

"We begin by noting the major difficulties that might attend dependence on foreign supplies:

1) War might possibly increase our petroleum requirements beyond the ability or willingness of foreign sources to supply us.
2) In a prolonged conventional war, the enemy might sink the tankers needed to import oil or to carry it to market from domestic production sources such as Alaska.
3) Local or regional revolution, hostilities, or guerilla activities might physically interrupt foreign production or transportation.
4) Exporting countries might be taken over by radical governments unwilling to do business with us or our allies.
5) Communist countries might induce exporting countries to deny their oil to the West.
6) A group of exporting countries might act in concert to deny their oil to us, as occurred briefly in the wake of the 1967 Arab-Israeli war.
7) Exporting countries might take over the assets of American or European companies.
8) Exporting countries might form an effective cartel raising oil prices substantially."[12]

Much of the report is taken up with a consideration of a number of possible crises of supply, the most likely one being a "group boycott" by middle eastern and north African oil producing nations against the U.S. and its allies.[13] The most extreme case examined is that in which the U.S. is cut off from all eastern hemisphere and Latin American oil, with only Canada as a secure source of supply.[14]

Throughout the report Canada is assumed to be the safest source of foreign supply, both because the country is politically secure and because its oil is available mainly through overland transport which is safer militarily than transport by sea.

"The risk of political instability or animosity is generally conceded to be very low in Canada. The risk of physical interruption or diversion of Canadian oil to other export markets in an emergency is also minimal for those deliveries made by inland transport", says the report.[15]

The only problem with Canada, in the view of the task force, is that the Canadian market east of the Ottawa valley is supplied by vulnerable overseas oil. Therefore, the overall policy of the U.S. should be to pressure Canada into closing this security hole as a precondition to entering into a complete energy deal with Canada:

"A large U.S. tariff preference for Canadian oil is difficult to justify while Eastern Canada continues to import all of its requirements from potentially insecure sources. In case of a supply interruption, Canada could be expected to turn to the United States to furnish those imports, or to compete for whatever supply is available, and thereby to subtract from the security value of U.S. imports from Western Canada. Some provision for limiting or offsetting Canadian vulnerability to an interruption of its own oil imports should therefore be made a precondition to unrestricted entry of Canadian oil into our market. Full realization of the security benefits implicit in such a preferential arrangement is also dependent on the development of common or harmonized United States-Canadian policies with respect to pipeline and other modes of transportation, access to natural gas, and other related energy matters. Pending the outcome of discussions on these subjects, the United States must decide what arrangements it is prepared to make unilaterally."[16]

Provided that Canada entered into a general deal with the United States on energy resources, the U.S. oil market would quickly be opened up to Canadian crude. Beginning with a level of 615,000 barrels a day[17] (the present level under the quota of March 1970, is 395,000 barrels a day), Canadian crude would be imported at a rate of 2 million barrels a day by 1975.[18] The latter figure would represent two-thirds of Canadian production by that date compared with the export of about 45 per cent of our production now.[19]

Naturally one thing the Americans don't like about sharply increasing their oil imports is that it will hurt their balance of payments position. For this reason it is considered important by the authors of the Shultz report that imports come as much as possible from countries where the industry has a high degree of American ownership, where the industry is likely to purchase equipment from the United States and where greater access to the local market for U.S. goods is possible.[20] As the report says "the economic infrastructure of the United States is and can be far more integrated with that of Canada than with the economy of any other country in the western hemisphere."[21] Anyone who imagines that a greatly increased sale of our oil to the United States can take place without great pressures for us to purchase more American industrial and manufactured goods should ponder the conclusion of the task force carefully. Obviously the supposed benefits of the energy deal in terms of jobs and tax dollars begin to vanish if it would bring in its train simply larger remittances of profits to the U.S. and greater imports of U.S. goods — goods which if manufactured in Canada would provide far more jobs and tax revenue than the export of raw products. The relationship between raw materials exports from the hinterland country and the import of finished goods from the metropolis is not lost on the task force; it should not be lost on Canadians either.

The separate report authored by Hickel, Stans, and Nassikas is as emphatic in stressing American security needs and the desirability of an energy deal with Canada, as is the main report. The separate report states:

"The pre-eminent position of the United States in the world depends in large part on the uninterrupted flow of oil and its products to its armed forces and civilian economy."[22]

Therefore, the separate report concludes:

"The United States should work diligently with Canada to reach a continental energy policy that assures our mutual security. Such a policy should cover energy broadly, and should deal with not only oil but natural gas, coal and hydro-electric and nuclear sources. Pending agreement on such a policy, which may take several years to negotiate, Canada and the United States should develop an effective mechanism to permit an orderly growth of imports of oil and natural gas from Canada."[23]

The Shultz report serves notice on Canada that a continental energy deal is seen as indispensable to U.S. security by all the elements in the present administration in Washington. Clearly once Canada makes such a deal, she can on no account be permitted to commit any of the sins outlined in the report as dangerous to the U.S. such as establishing public ownership of her resource industries, or even seeking better terms of trade for her resources throughout the world.

During the 1956 middle east oil crisis, U.S. Secretary of State, John Foster Dulles met with the presidents of American oil firms. He told them his attitude to nationalization of U.S. corporations by foreign governments. This is the record of his statement as taken down by one of the executives present:

". . . the United States would not acquiesce in the rights of nationalization that would affect any other facilities in our own economic interests . . . He commented that international law recognizes the right to nationalize if adequate compensation is paid, but he admits that actually adequate compensation is never really paid and nationalization, in effect, thereby becomes confiscation . . . the United States felt it was O.K. to nationalize only if assets were not impressed with international interest. What he meant by international interest was where a foreign government had made promises of fixed duration in the form of concessions or contracts, upon which other nations would rely on fixing their courses of action and their own economies . . . Therefore . . . nationalization of this kind of an asset impressed with international interest goes far beyond compensation of shareholders alone, and should call for international intervention."[24]

The energy deal will make it imperative for Canada to be allowed no future freedom of action in deciding what to do with her energy resources.

While even long term military alliances can eventually be abrogated, an energy deal which makes the U.S. dependent on Canadian sources of supply will be a truly "perpetual alliance" guaranteeing to Canadians perpetual colonialism. The CIA-planned coup in Greece reveals the lengths to which the United States is willing to go to make sure that an "ally" does not act in ways that are seen as contrary to American national security.

IV WATER - NEXT ON THE AGENDA

Looming behind the power shortage and the energy shortage in general, is the resource question that both American and Canadian officials want to keep quiet about, until the preliminary deals have been made – the water question. There is no doubt that water is the ultimate energy resource and that the availability of plentiful, fresh water is the key to modern industry. The U.S. has been feeling the water pinch acutely for over half a decade, both in terms of pollution and absolute shortages, particularly in the south-west of the United States.

There is little doubt that once the U.S. successfully gains access to our oil and natural gas on its terms, it will turn to our water.

In 1964 Canadians were treated to a garish glimpse of their possible future in a North America in which their water was to be treated as a "continental" resource. In that year the Frank M. Parsons Company of Los Angeles unveiled what it called the North American Water and Power Alliance.

A thirsty U.S. Congressman, Jim Wright, in a book entitled *The Coming Water Famine,* outlined the main ingredients of the NAWAPA plan as follows:

"The NAWAPA idea consists, first, of building huge dams in Alaska and the Canadian Yukon to trap the abundant water of the various broad rivers in those areas, where the resource is little needed. . . .

"The program calls for (hold your hats!) conducting the waters into a largely man-made reservoir *five hundred miles long,* using the natural gorge of the Rocky Mountain Trench. In order to do this, it will be necessary to build a series of connecting tunnels, canals, lakes, dams and even lifts.

"At the northern end of the Trench, NAWAPA proposes to dredge a thirty-foot-deep canal all the way to Lake Superior, supplying the Great Lakes with the fresh water they so badly need. Another division of the canal would feed water into the upper stretches of the Mississippi and Missouri Rivers.

"A series of dams and power stations would lift the water up to the three-thousand-foot altitude of the Rocky Mountain Trench, a natural geological defile in southwestern (sic) British Columbia, from five to fifteen miles wide, which stretches for a length of about nine hundred miles. The site for the big storage reservoir would be the five hundred down-stream miles of the southern end of the Trench.

"From the Trench Reservoir water would be pump-lifted to the Sawtooth Reservoir in northwestern Montana. From this point, the water would flow southward by gravity, via lined canals and tunnels, throughout the western part of the system, passing the Sawtooth Mountain barrier through a tunnel eighty feet in diameter and fifty miles in length.

"This water would help mightily to meet the needs of the western states for irrigation, industry, power, recreation, and municipal conservation."[1]

One might imagine that a scheme that proposed to tear out the water system of a neighbouring country, wreak indescribable havoc on much of that country's ecology and flood a vast part of the interior of one province of that country would be dismissed as lunacy. But such is the American thirst for water and sense of imperial grandeur that the NAWAPA scheme was taken with terrifying seriousness.

Congressman Wright was moved to patriotic raptures at the mere thought of the plan. He wrote:

"This dream is, admittedly, both grandiose and visionary. However, the nation was built by visionaries. There have been some disturbing indications in recent years that we may have lost some of our capacity for dreaming and acting in those areas concerning our survival upon this earth."[2]

When the scheme came before a Senate Subcommittee, Senator Frank Church of Idaho proclaimed:

"Whether or not this proposal is advanced further, whether or not it is adopted, we must not be deterred by its size. To perform the great task before us may well need a program as farsighted as was the Louisiana Purchase."[3]

In 1966 in an address to the Royal Society of Canada shortly before his death, General A. G. L. McNaughton who had been chairman of the Canadian section of the Internation Joint

Commission took up the cudgels against NAWAPA in a strongly worded reply to Utah Senator Frank Moss's defence of the scheme. McNaughton stated:

"The NAWAPA propagandists love to talk of great quantities of water spilling unused into the Arctic Ocean. But the major sources for the scheme are hundreds of miles from the Arctic Ocean. They are in fact the rivers of the Canadian Cordillera, which provide a great series of prime power sites; rivers which form the basis of one of the world's great concentrations of the forest products industry; rivers which provide some of the finest salmon runs in the world. There are detailed plans on Canadian drawing-boards, and there are projects now under construction to harness these flows. The associated mineral and forest resources are already staked out, and the required human and financial resources are being attracted to the region. The NAWAPA promoters would move all of this out of Canada — the people, the industry, the water. It can only be described as madness to believe that Canada has surplus water in an area that is so obviously earmarked for major resource development, and where so much activity to that end is already taking place.

"Of course, NAWAPA has nothing to do with the maximum development of these rivers or resources in Canada. Its purpose is to flood the valleys in Canada, and to drain off the water in regulated flow for beneficial use in the United States. But the valleys themselves are of vital importance to British Columbia, because they contain the level land which is so vitally needed for roads and railways, for industries, for people, and for agriculture. Whitehorse and Prince George would be submerged, and their land with them, as would countless miles of railway and highway. These irreplaceable assets would be destroyed in the name of trans-mountain navigation.

"In my address to the Canadian Club in Montreal in October, 1965, I referred to some of the serious legal and political implications of the NAWAPA scheme. I observed at that time that this is a monstrous concept, not only in terms of physical magnitude, but also in another and more sinister sense, in that the promoters would displace Canadian sovereignty over the national waters of Canada, and substitute there for a diabolic thesis that *all* waters of North America become a shared resource, of which most will be drawn off for the benefit of the midwest and southwest regions of the United States, where existing desert areas will be made to bloom at the expense of development in Canada.

". . . To me it is obvious that if we make a bargain to divert water to the United States, we cannot ever discontinue or we shall face force to compel compliance. There is nothing in our experience to date which indicates any change in the vigour with which our American friends pursue objectives which they deem in their national interests, however much this may hurt a neighbour who has unwittingly made a careless bargain in other circumstances."[4]

It has been becoming clear during the past few years that the idea that Canada has great quantities of surplus water that can be exported is merely a myth — and a highly dangerous one. In its projections of energy supply to 1990, the National Energy Board estimated that whereas hydro sources accounted for 82 per cent of the generation of electricity in 1966, this would drop to 45 per cent by 1990. For Ontario the figures are even more striking: hydro sources accounted for over 70 per cent of production in 1966; by 1990 this would drop to 20 per cent. The fact that the National Energy Board is predicting a massive shift to thermal and nuclear generation of electricity, shows that there is, in fact, no vast surplus of water in Canada that could be exported without creating difficulty.

In an article in *Foreign Affairs* in July 1970, geographer Trevor Lloyd further punctures the myth of Canada's exportable water:

"Fresh water is a renewable resource that is attracting increasing attention in the drier parts of North America where the supplies have been polluted or depleted. The landscape of much of the far north includes a rich variety of lakes, ponds and rivers and gives an impression of providing a reserve of water which might become available for use elsewhere. The impression is misleading. Precipitation over much of the North is low, although evaporation is also low and the permafrost beneath prevents the water from draining away. While information is still incomplete, it suggests that the northern water reserves can contribute little or nothing for export southward."[5]

Since the genesis of the NAWAPA idea, a much greater awareness has grown up in both Canada and the United States of the danger of environmental damage from various kinds of resource use. An example of this heightened sensitivity is revealed by the opposition of American conservationists to the building of a 48 inch oil pipeline through Alaska permafrost at temperatures of 160 degrees fahrenheit.[6] The threat posed by the diversion of major water supplies from the north is much more serious than is the danger of northern pipelines.

In spite of this rising fear of environmental damage the Canadian government is in a vulnerable position when it comes to protecting Canadian water resources from an increasingly thirsty United States. Even after taking into consideration the immense power that the United States government can bring to bear on Canada on any matter, it remains difficult to understand what can only appear the complete incompetence or wilful neglect of Canadian interests when it comes to water.

The Canadian government goes into any negotiations with the U.S. on water much weaker than would have been the case a decade ago. The incredible bungling that surrounded the Columbia River Treaty which came into effect in 1964 gave weight to the concept of developing Canadian water as a continental resource in sharp contrast to earlier negotiations about water under the auspices of the International Joint Commission. When the International Joint Commission was established in 1909, it operated as a Canadian-American body consisting of two national sections, each with three members headed by a chairman, as the machinery for resolving differences between the two countries.[7] Underlying the I.J.C. was the assumption that there would be conflicts between the two nations on the question of the boundary waters and that an international agency was needed to resolve the differences.

The key doctrine in deciding disputes was the Harmon doctrine which asserted that the upstream country has an unfettered right to "exclusive jurisdiction and control over the use and diversion . . . of waters on its own side of the line which in their natural channels would flow across the boundary or into boundary waters." Furthermore the downstream state, without the approval of the IJC is prevented from construction of any works on the river which would cause the natural level of waters to be raised on the other side of the boundary.[8] While the Harmon doctrine favors the United States in its dealings with Mexico and on the eastern half of the continent, it favors Canada for most rivers of significance which cross the boundary on the western part of the continent.

The Columbia River Treaty dispenses with the principle of separate national development of the boundary waters. In spite of the fact that Canada is the upstream state in the case of the Columbia, the major benefits and future decision making regarding the Columbia basin has been arrogated to the United States. As

Larratt Higgins points out, "It will cost Canada about $100 million to give the Columbia away, to say nothing of the cost of losing the International Joint Commission as an effective means of protecting Canadian rights elsewhere."[9]

In spite of the fact that the Treaty explicitly states that no precedent has been set by the principles embodied in it, it is obvious that the Treaty is a standing invitation to the U.S. to regard Canadian water as continental water. The Columbia Treaty not only weakened the position of Canada in future dealings with the United States, it also managed to weaken the position of the Canadian federal government vis a vis the provinces. Because it was British Columbia that pressured for the treaty against a weak-kneed federal government, Ottawa was made to appear as a mere agency of the province in determining the Canadian interest with respect to boundary waters.

In August, 1964, a statement by the Western Canadian-American Assembly held at Harrison Hot Springs, B.C., under the auspices of the University of British Columbia and Columbia University pointed to the future that the Columbia River Treaty opened up for Canada. The report stated:

"Canada and the United States are moving in the direction of a new and significant policy for the development of energy resources, particularly water power, on a continental scale. Recent technological advances which have made the border increasingly irrelevant have brought about in both countries a willingness to consider an encouraging degree of integration . . ."[10]

The past three Canadian Prime Ministers have each contributed to the impending catastrophe regarding Canadian water. Diefenbaker, in spite of his supposed Canadian nationalism, managed to blunder his way into the Columbia River agreement. Not a man to do things by halves, Diefenbaker proclaimed the Columbia River Treaty a great advance for mankind. At the signing ceremony he directed the following remarks to President Eisenhower:

"Mr. President, this, I believe, is an historic milestone in Canadian-American relations. As you have said, this project is one of the greatest projects that has ever been undertaken. Indeed, it is the first occasion in history when two nations, side by side, have agreed to the distribution of power as between their two countries and the sharing of the development of an international river to the same extent as will be the result in the years ahead.

"And as you have said, this relationship between our countries is something that is a model for all mankind. Indeed, it would be difficult to understand the relationship between our two countries when placed alongside the relationships that prevail between other countries in the world today. My hope is that, in the years ahead, this day will be looked back on as one that represents the greatest advance that has ever been made in international relations between countries."[11]

Lester Pearson, who at first appeared to be opposed to the Columbia deal, managed to make the following ill-advised statement on television during the 1965 election:

"The United States is finding that water is one of its most valuable and is becoming one of its scarcest resources . . . the question of water resources . . . is a continental and international problem. We have to be careful not to alienate this resource without taking care of our own needs and we will be discussing this with the United States who are very anxious to work out arrangements by which some of our water resources are moved down south. This can be as important as exporting wheat or oil."[12]

Not to be outdone, Prime Minister Trudeau managed in February, 1970, to add his own distinctive contribution to the water debacle. His timing was splendid in its irony. On the same day that J. J. Greene was attempting to polish his image by telling the House of Commons that Canada was not considering exporting water to the U.S., Trudeau went on the TV show "Under Attack" at Carleton University. In response to an accusation by a student that the government was about to sell Canadian water, Trudeau made the following reply about resources in general, including water:

"I don't want to be a dog in the manger about this. But if people are not going to use it, can't we sell it for good hard cash?"[13]

On the same occasion, apparently oblivious to the possible effects of his statements on Canada's bargaining position, the Prime Minister warned that if we were too possessive of our gas and oil, we might never be able to use these resources and might find ourselves "locked in the oil and petroleum age."[14]

In July, 1970, the prospect of American pressure for Canadian water came into public view again. The Canadian Water Resources Association was told that by 1980 the United States will be short an estimated 50 billion to 100 billion gallons of water a year, if other sources aren't found. In a statement whose assertiveness will hardly suffice to make up for the bungling of three Canadian Prime

Ministers, Bud Orange, parliamentary secretary to J. J. Greene, told the meeting on water resources that there is "no way" Canada will allow the sale of its water to the United States.[15] To underline his remarks, Orange said he was speaking for the federal government. That may well be, but presumably Diefenbaker, Pearson and Trudeau were also speaking on behalf of the federal government, were they not?

General McNaughton was right in stressing the point that once you turn on the tap and begin supplying the Americans with water, you dare not ever turn it off. After all, even Fidel Castro stopped short of shutting off the water mains that supply fresh water to the American naval base at Guantanamo.

V RESISTING THE ENERGY DEAL

Calgary is a city whose sense of community, of history, of self-direction was shattered by a single event — the discovery of oil in Alberta and the takeover of Alberta's oil industry by American oil companies. As effectively as the atomic blast at Hiroshima forced the building of a new city, the oil industry created its own new environment, built on the devastated ruins of the old city of Calgary. In the period before the rise of oil, Calgary had been a centre for lively and powerful political and social movements. It had possessed a tough tradition of independent journalism; it was an intellectual centre for the activities of the movement that brought the United Farmers of Alberta to power in the provincial election of 1921; its maverick MP's at Ottawa contributed to the formation of the ginger group that underlay the formation of the CCF — in fact, the first national meeting to launch the CCF was held in Calgary in 1932; and, of course, Calgary was the home of William Aberhart's Prophetic Bible Institute, from which he launched the Social Credit movement. All this is not to glorify Calgary as a major fount of civilization, but simply to point out the vitality and innovation of the community before it became the branch office of a monopoly-controlled extractive industry.

Calgary died socially and politically as a community with the rise of oil. The sterility, brutality and crass materialism of Texas and Oklahoma were stamped on the city and the local culture did not have sufficient strength to resist the city's new masters. It went under, and since that time the city has existed for no other reason than for the greater good of the oil industry and the bounties that it distributes locally.

The glitter of the city's new concrete and glass towers and its thousands of acres of new North American suburbia cannot cover up the fact that almost no one in Calgary dares to raise a whisper of criticism about the direction of the industry that has the community in its grip. Calgary's previous culture had no ingredient to protect itself against the mindless materialism and dependency that the foreign owned oil industry brought — that's why the old culture is now extinct. At the moment, there is no politics in Calgary. When political controversy returns, it will be of the savage variety, that is produced when the victims of the truncated cultural, political and social system strike out in fury at the system. Calgary will lie dormant for a time and then it will explode.

Calgary should be a warning and a representation to all Canada of the road ahead for a society that allows itself to be reduced to the prostitution of living largely as a resource extractor for another society. Canada as a whole has been suffocated by this reality throughout its history. In Calgary the process has reached its logical conclusion, with the death of the community.

The way in which the Canadian political system at the national level has responded to the question of the continental energy resources deal reveals the muting of our politics that flows from our colonial dependency as a raw materials exporter. There has been a banal lack of concern for the most part in dealing with a proposed giveaway of resources that is staggering. Our political system is so attuned to dependency that it cannot but be prosaic in the face of events which will shape the entire future of the Canadian people. The fact that there is so little instinct for self-preservation in established Canadian politics reveals how close the system as a whole is to the graveyard that Calgary has already found.

The technocracy of the Liberals, the numbness of the Conservatives — this is the muted politics of colonialism. The so-called debate on foreign ownership limps forward in the mainstream of the political system as though what was at stake was the fate of several counties and not the fate of half a continent.

Beneath the surface of established politics, though, the rage against the sell-out of Canada grows. On every hand people are rejecting the idea that we have no choice but to serve as a resource base and consumer market of American imperialism. There is a new sense of power among the Canadian people — a sense of possibility. The old political system in this country is living in its last days. A storm is coming in English Canada of the kind that has shaken Quebec for the past ten years and any institution, party, government or leadership that does not understand this will be swept aside.

The energy deal and the continentalization of Canadian resources concretizes the politics of anti-imperialism in this country. It now becomes clear that the dependency of Canada leads not to a quieter life in our corner of the world, but to a transformation of the environment itself, which turns our country into a giant supplier for the industrial system of the United States. This means fewer and less interesting jobs for Canadians in the long run; it means potentially immense damage to the Canadian environment as our oil and gas and water is removed from the north with its delicate ecological system; it means almost total political powerlessness for Canadians as they are doomed to life in a permanent hinterland. And tragically the destruction of Canada would not even mean salvation for the United States. It would merely add more time during which the United States could carry on its wasteful and rapacious existence. But the problem of coming to terms with the environment will not be solved for America through the rape of Canada.

The stark threat which faces Canadians makes the political expressions which we have had in our national politics largely irrelevant. A new Canada and a new Canadian politics will be born out of the struggle that must be joined to make possible a society in Canada, in which our resources serve people both at home and abroad and in which the people who work in the industries of the country determine the direction of the economy and receive its benefits.

In Ottawa the old politics of tinkering with continental capitalism continues. On July 27, 1970 the House of Commons committee on External Affairs and National Defence recommended that Canada move toward 51 per cent Canadian ownership of all corporations in the country. Within 24 hours of the proposal, the business community was howling its disapproval and the chairman of the commons committee, Ian Wahn, was expressing doubts. Wahn said the 51 per cent recommendation "may never be enacted — perhaps it wouldn't even be practical."[1]

The important thing to understand in debates about whether the percentage of American ownership of Canadian corporations is reduced to be replaced with Canadian corporate ownership, is that it makes very little difference to the behaviour of the firms. There is no doubt that given the present structure of the Canadian economy and given private ownership, of whatever nationality, resource producing corporations in Canada will seek a continental resources deal with the United States. Whether the companies are Canadian owned or not, they will pursue policies which will lead to Canada's increased dependence on raw material exports, the effect of which will be to heighten the unemployment problem and to lead to a long term trend away from economic diversification of Canada's economy. The results of this policy will be disastrous in terms of quality of life, available jobs and capacity of Canadians to make their own political decisions. So far gone are we as a resource producing hinterland for U.S. capitalism that only a completely different approach to the development of the Canadian economy can allow us to break out of the present pattern.

The 51 per cent Canadian ownership model has been much touted of late by Walter Gordon and others as the Mexican method of avoiding foreign capitalist domination. The method is a sham. All it does is to assure domestic capitalists a bigger share of the pie. Colonialism stems from the structural relationship of a country's economy to metropolitan capitalist countries, and has little to do with the formal ownership pattern of the country's economy. There is little doubt that the American corporate interests in Canada will resist the 51 per cent demand in any case. But the important point is to realize that the entire debate about the 51 per cent plan is of marginal importance.

At present, it is clear that virtually any Canadian government that represents private corporate interests (Canadian and foreign) or any government that is not willing to struggle across the board against corporate interests (Canadian and foreign) will be forced by the logic of the present situation to enter into a long-term energy resources deal with the United States, either piece-meal or as a package. With such a deal will come a trend toward a more old-fashioned and blunt imperial relationship between the United States and Canada such as has always existed between the U.S. and Latin America. In their book, *Monopoly Capital,* Baran and Sweezy are quite right when they include all countries in Latin America except Cuba (they do include Mexico) in the American empire. Significantly their list also includes Canada and one European country, Greece.[2]

Baran and Sweezy also summarize the wants of American corporations in dealing with foreign countries:

"What they want is *monopolistic control* over foreign sources of supply and foreign markets, enabling them to buy and sell on specially privileged terms, to shift orders from one subsidiary to another, to favour this country or that depending on which has the most advantageous tax, labor, and other policies — in a word, they want to do business on their own terms and wherever they choose. And for this what they need is not trading partners but 'allies' and clients willing to adjust their laws and policies to the requirements of American big business."[3]

It is overwhelmingly apparent that the U.S. will only allow itself to become dependent on Canadian oil and natural gas *provided that our supplies are absolutely dependable in exactly the same way that U.S. domestic supplies are.* This means an energy deal will only come about if the Canadian government agrees never to interfere with the resource sector of the Canadian economy. U.S. conglomerates must dictate the price and must continue to hold overwhelming ownership of the Canadian resource industries. The energy deal demands a handing over of Canadian sovereignty that is no less great than Panama's lease of the canal zone to the U.S.

The ultimate fear of the U.S. in its relationship with resource extracting countries is of nationalization of American corporate holdings. Before any deal is concluded, it will have to be made perfectly clear that the Canadian government is waiving its right to bring the vital resource sector under public ownership. In a very real sense, we are being asked to take an oath to uphold unrestricted free enterprise for all time if we make such a deal. The energy deal, far more than most sections of the BNA Act will define the future powers of the Canadian government. It will mark a formal return to colonial status.

These limitations should prove no hardship for the Liberal party, though. This is the third time in the past century that the Liberals have tried to achieve free trade in raw materials with the United States. And, of course, the Liberals will not really notice having their sovereignty limited to orthodox free enterprise, since they have never been inclined to question its limits in any case.

Of course, there are many men of letters in this country who are still debating whether there is significant American control of Canada. They have not yet perceived the main course of Canadian history, let alone the possible alternatives for the Canadian future. Many of them will undoubtedly fail to recognize that the energy deal is coming. Once it comes they will not understand its implications. An inability to perceive the reality of conditions in one's country is quite naturally, endemic to colonialism.

The impending energy deal forces the Canadian people to face up to fundamentals in contemplating their future course. It will mark a genuine parting of the ways for Canada. To resist the energy deal, means breaking fundamentally with past social and economic developments in Canada. Canadian capitalists and their governments cannot avoid the energy deal because their whole history has led them to it. At this point in Canada it becomes clear that only socialism provides an alternative path that can lead us out of the political dependency and economic underdevelopment that is our fate under the present system.

Only through a strategy of using the resources in Canada to develop and diversify the Canadian economy can this country ensure all of its people jobs and control of their lives socially and politically. Surpluses of resources in Canada should be exported only after the resource needs for this kind of strategy have been amply planned for. Canadian resources should be consciously seen as a tool for freeing us from the control of the American Empire. The Liberals see Canadian resources as a means of gaining a better deal for Canadian business within the American Empire. Their strategy leads to an intensification of the key historic problem with the Canadian economy — the vulnerability and rigidity that stems from dependence on a small number of staple exports.

A wholly different strategy is required if Canada is to experience balanced and diversified economic development in the interest of its people. Only public ownership and public control of the resource industries can break us out of the pattern of dependency and comparative underdevelopment that has been endemic to Canada. Repatriation of the Canadian economy should begin at its centre — the resource sector. Public ownership of the resource industries would place the key sector of our economy in the hands of the people. It would give Canadians the opportunity to master the skills necessary to run our economy and *to develop it qualitatively in the interests of human well-being in Canada.*

Canada could then industrialize in the resource producing areas, which have long been seen merely as sources of raw materials. The wealth that comes out of the ground in the countless Canadian mining towns would be channeled to diversifying the economy of the resource producing areas, so that people there could pursue a wide variety of activities and occupations.

And then we must come to terms with the environment itself. Mankind has need of the bounties of this planet for a long time to come. A resource policy that is geared to that future and not to immediate profit is essential, if we are to survive. In dealing with this problem we will have to think in world terms. We must work out ways of recycling resources that have already been taken from the ground. We must place a limit on certain kinds of mindless growth that gravely compromise the future of humanity.

When we are told that in a few years, three hundred jumbo jets will be using seven per cent of the oil produced annually in the world, is it not time to ask what limits should be placed on the spoliation of our planet? Because Canada is relatively resource rich, Canadians must see their resources as a holding for all mankind. Instead of serving a corporate and military empire with those resources, we must plan for their long run use to benefit humanity at home and abroad.

The resource question touches all Canadians, individually and as a people. Canada's resources, the centre of our activity historically, have also been the centre of our common experience. If our resources have been the key to our dependency, they are also the key to our liberation. Following the Columbia River Treaty, critics said that such a thing must never be allowed to happen again. It *is* happening again on a much larger scale. This time the key political factor will be the extent of resistance to the deal *before* the event and the determination of Canadians not to recognize as legitimate the commitments that are about to be made in their name by the government.

i The Merchant-Heeny Report

from *Canadian-American Relations,* Vol. 1, 1867–1967. U.S. Information Service, U.S. Embassy, Ottawa, Nov. 1967.

Guidelines for Consultation

54. We now turn to the essence of consultation and to certain guidelines which, in our judgment, should be observed by our two governments in their dealings with each other:

(a) In the first place, every effort should be made to begin the consultative process sufficiently early to provide reasonable time for each party to consider and give full weight to the views and interests of the other. This will help to satisfy each side that its position on any issue is being seriously examined. It will also improve the chances of resolving difficulties and, where no detours around roadblocks are to be found, it can ease the shock of impending collision.

(b) In certain fields where combined efforts are called for, such as continental air defence arrangements and joint development of resources, there is obvious advantage in having the consultative process begin at the planning stage so as to facilitate concurrent formulation of policy.

(c) There will be in the future — as in the past — cases where, by reason of what is deemed an overriding need for speed or secrecy, the process of consultation must be telescoped. This is a fact of life which must be recognized, but the judgment in such circumstances should be that of the highest authority.

(d) While all crises are not predictable, many — probably most — can be foreseen as possible. For this reason the process of consultation should provide for continuous exchanges of views between the appropriate authorities of the two governments over the whole range of looming problems, including mutual exposure to any relevant contingency planning.

(e) Consultation should be initiated whenever one of the two governments is in the process of formulating important policies or planning actions which would have an appreciable impact on the other. The responsibility for initiating consultation in such cases rests on the party approaching decision or contemplating action.

(f) Existing mechanisms for consultation should be utilized in order to ensure prompt and continuous access by one government to the other.

(g) Many problems between our two governments are susceptible of solution only through the quiet, private and patient examination of facts in the search for accommodation. It should be regarded as incumbent on both parties during this time-consuming process to avoid, so far as possible, the adoption of public positions which can contribute unnecessarily to public division and difference.

(h) Each government has a responsibility to ensure that its own procedure for intragovernmental consideration of subjects which affect the other country operates promptly, effectively and consistently so as to facilitate the consultative process.

55. We recognize that the kind of consultation which we have described has different implications for our respective governments. These derive primarily from the wide disparity in power and international responsibility which we have already underlined. In consultations with the United States, Canadian authorities must have confidence that the practice of quiet diplomacy is not only neighbourly and convenient to the United States but that it is in fact more effective than the alternative of raising a row and being unpleasant in public. By the same token, the United States authorities must be satisfied that, in such consultations, Canada will have sympathetic regard for the world-wide preoccupations and responsibilities of the United States.

56. Such a regime of consultation is difficult — for both sides — but we are convinced that it is fundamental to the maintenance of healthy relations between our two governments and peoples. We believe it can be most effective in the best interests of both if it is conducted along the above lines.

Projects for Partnership

63. If such fundamentals be accepted on both sides, then the border need prove no barrier or hindrance to a common approach, as partners, in broad areas of the national lives of the two countries. Indeed, this has already been demonstrated in many ways over many years, for example, in the great joint enterprise of the St. Lawrence Seaway and Power Project and in the agreement for the co-operative development of the water resources of the Columbia River Basin.

A. Energy

64. We have been impressed by the prospects of mutual benefit which might be realized in closer co-operation and coordination between our two countries in the production and distribution of energy, especially electrical energy. Under appropriate conditions, joint planning and development of resources to that end in various regions would appear to afford promising opportunities. For this reason we recommend early and serious study of such possibilities.

65. We have been led to this conclusion by a number of circumstances in the current and prospective situation:

(a) the high and rapidly rising use of energy in the two countries and its increasing importance to our peoples and in the economic development of the regions in which they live;

(b) recent technological advances, especially in extra-high voltage transmission, which create the potential for substantial future reductions in costs;

(c) the economic advantages to both countries of disregarding the boundary for energy purposes, that is, in the development and distribution of energy on a regional north-south basis where this is to the mutual advantage. Such an approach permits the "economies of scale" to operate to reduce costs; planning can be coordinated and efficient; and mutually profitable interchanges and interconnections can be effected, taking advantage of the different time zones and the diversity of climatic conditions which can produce important savings.

66. In any such study, and in any subsequent co-operative arrangements worked out between the competent authorities in the two countries, a number of important points would have to be kept in mind:

(a) the differing situation as between the various sources of energy and their changing importance relative to one another;

(b) the importance of having regard to whole north-south regions at an early stage in the design and development of networks;

(c) the need to establish jointly in advance that significant net benefits would result from joint projects, and that such benefits could be equitably divided;

(d) the wisdom of avoiding situations in which the entities involved in one country become in effect "public utilities" in the other; and,

(e) the protection of the national interests of each country.

67. Primary responsibility for moving ahead, and much of the expertise, particularly in electricity, rests with the system-owners — public and private — in the two countries, and much of the authority resides elsewhere, notably within State and Provincial jurisdiction. Nevertheless, we are persuaded that in this area there is opportunity for advantageous co-operative leadership and initiative in the two national governments.

68. We appreciate the variety of differing circumstances which affect the various energy sources in the two countries. There are, for example, special conditions bearing on coal, oil and gas which are not all or equally applicable to electrical energy. Nevertheless, we believe there would be virtue in having a joint look at the energy picture as a whole.

69.   We express no opinion as to how such studies can best be undertaken and advanced, whether under the aegis of a joint body or by the coordinated efforts of the appropriate elements and agencies of government in the two countries.

ii The Shultz Report

The Oil Import Question: A Report on the Relationship of Oil Imports to the National Security. By the Cabinet Task Force on Oil Import Control. Washington, Feb. 1970.

211. Kinds of risks. To facilitate the following brief discussion, we begin by noting the major difficulties that might attend dependence on foreign supplies. (1) War might possibly increase our petroleum requirements beyond the ability or willingness of foreign sources to supply us. (2) In a prolonged conventional war, the enemy might sink the tankers needed to import oil or to carry it to market from domestic production sources such as Alaska. (3) Local or regional revolution, hostilities, or guerilla activities might physically interrupt foreign production or transportation. (4) Exporting countries might be taken over by radical governments unwilling to do business with us or our allies. (5) Communist countries might induce exporting countries to deny their oil to the West. (6) A group of exporting countries might act in concert to deny their oil to us, as occurred briefly in the wake of the 1967 Arab-Israeli war. (7) Exporting countries might take over the assets of American or European companies. (8) Exporting countries might form an effective cartel raising oil prices substantially.

213. Other consuming countries enter our analysis in three ways.

213a. Pooled supplies. A country supplying oil in an emergency would insist on the satisfaction of its own needs. If, for example, we count on Venezuelan oil as secure in an emergency, we must aggregate Venezuelan consumption (and that of its Latin American customers) with our own to determine the gross need to be met. We must consider treating Canada this way in light of its oil policy admitting unrestricted imports into the eastern provinces. To be sure, Canada now has no pipeline permitting it to divert Western supplies to Eastern consumption. In an emergency, however, our own oil might be called on to supply the needs of Eastern Canada — offsetting to that extent the U.S. security benefits of the oil Canada ships to us from its West.

214. Producing countries. (a) Diversity. In 1956, there were four major oil exporters. Today, there are at least potentially eleven and the number is growing, extending from the Arab and non-Arab countries of the Middle East through North Africa and West Africa to the Caribbean and on to Indonesia. Although any one of these sources may experience political crises or physical disruptions over the next decade, there is little likelihood that such upheavals would take place in all or most of the exporting countries simultaneously. The growing number and diversity of their locations and interests also make it more difficult to achieve a prolonged concerted boycott for political or economic ends. It must of course be recognized that most of the growth in oil production has thus far occurred in the Arab states, with implications that require and are given separate attention below.

214b. Oil revenues needed. Most exporting countries, moreover, need their hard-currency oil revenues (or the equivalent) to finance internal economic development and military requirements. Expectations generated by such revenues are difficult to stifle for any extended period, although it must be recognized that some individual countries have in the past foregone revenues for several years for political reasons. Generally speaking, however, every producing country wants to sell more oil.

214c. An intermediate proposition. In view of this combination of diversity of source and need for oil revenues, we would not find it probable that "most" producing countries would deny their oil to most consuming countries for a "prolonged" period. Nevertheless, concentration of much of the world's oil in an area characterized by high tension does pose risks. And the risk that is not declared probable may nevertheless be real enough to warrant expenditures to guard against it.

Particular Interruptions

215. Middle East uncertainties. So long as tensions continue in the area, several problems with Middle Eastern supplies may be noted.

215a. Physical disruption. In the event of another regional war, it is not inconceivable that major Arab oil installations might be attacked. Incidental interdiction of Iranian delivery routes is also possible. A physical disruption attributable to a regional war is not likely to be long – probably not more than a few months – but we cannot exclude the possibility of prolonged interruption. Sporadic guerilla activity – short of regional war – is not likely to interrupt the bulk of exports.

215b. Concerted political denial. It is possible that the Arab states might band together as they did briefly in 1967 to ban oil shipments to specified Western countries. If the boycott were brief or were directed selectively against only one or two importing countries, total supply would remain adequate. Thus to have a problem, one must postulate something approaching a total denial to all markets of all or most Arab oil. The probable duration of any such concerted action may, however, be limited by the difficulty of maintaining political cohesion in the face of sacrifice of immediately needed revenues and the risk of losing market share to exporters not participating in the boycott. Still, given the tensions in the area, the possibility of a prolonged and virtually total boycott cannot be ignored. We will focus our planning hypotheses on a 12-month Arab supply interruption, while also considering the effects of a longer and broader denial.

216. Radical regimes; Soviet involvement. Hostile governments are unlikely to arise simultaneously in major supplying countries. There might, however, be a succession of such governments. In either case, such governments would need to market their petroleum. If they wished to deny supplies to the West, they would have to rely on the Soviet Union, itself a major producer and net exporter, to absorb large volumes of supplies diverted from the West, to finance diversion of such supplies to its allies, or otherwise to underwrite a broad-scale denial of such supplies. To do so, the Soviet Union would have to supply the hard currencies desired by the exporting countries or the equivalent in goods and services. In 1980, the Arab countries alone would be exporting something like 30 million barrels per day, with tax and royalty income of approximately $1 per barrel or more than $10 billion per year. To underwrite the denial of any substantial portion of these exports would be very costly indeed.

217. Venezuela. Venezuela and the neighboring islands have been steady large-scale suppliers to the U.S. market during World War II and in all subsequent circumstances. Civil strife or political upheaval of a sort that would disrupt Venezuelan supplies does not seem likely in the foreseeable future. Any interruption that might possibly occur would probably be short in view of the consensus among all Venezuelan factions in favor of selling oil to us. In a severe Eastern Hemisphere supply curtailment, however, and assuming that European countries have not made adequate provision for their own emergency needs, Venezuelan oil shipments might be diverted from the U.S. to Europe as a result either of premium price bidding or of conscious acquiescence on our part.

218. Other countries. The ties between Canada and the United States are close and the two countries have already recognized their energy inter-dependence in, for example, electrical interconnections. Most Latin American countries, apart from Venezuela, now have no significant export surplus for other than neighbouring countries. The remaining exporter nations, such as Nigeria and Indonesia – although they have experienced disruptions – in general add to the diversity that contributes to our security. New production is being developed at the same time in such areas as West Africa and Latin America.

219. Economic exploitation. The exporting countries might form an effective cartel that would charge us "a monopoly price." But that seems unlikely. Furthermore, the possibility of a monopoly price in the future is not usually a persuasive reason for paying an enhanced price now.

220. Nuclear war. A general war involving a large-scale nuclear exchange is considered unlikely. If it did occur, the continuity of oil supply would not likely be a matter of major significance. It is considered probable that production of crude oil would be in excess of actual consumption in a shattered economy in the aftermath of a nuclear exchange.

221. Limited war. Our experience in limited wars such as in Korea and Vietnam indicates that dependence on foreign oil supplies in limited wars does not lead to protracted supply interruptions.

222. General non-nuclear war is considered unlikely, but must be assessed in terms of the obvious need for oil to carry on such a war and the risks of interruption of supply that it would create.

224c. Implications. Submissions to the Task Force have suggested that a prolonged conventional war is a possibility but not a probability or the key risk. Nevertheless, to the extent that one wished to insure against a conventional war of longer duration than the political interruptions to be discussed, the distinctive implications of submarine risks must be stressed: (1) Domestic supplies — which import restrictions seek to increase — are not invulnerable to submarines, as we discovered during World War II when German submarines sank many tankers carrying oil from Gulf to Atlantic ports. Import restrictions do not bring us total insurance against submarines unless provision is made to supply the East and West Coasts from Gulf Coast and Alaskan sources by pipelines or other inland means of transportation. (2) Western Hemisphere oil on the other hand does provide incremental security, since in the view of the Defense Department the Caribbean and coastal waters affected during World War II are now significantly more secure than the high seas. To the extent that submarines are an anticipated problem, Venezuelan oil is no less secure than seaborne domestic oil. Similarly, Mexican and, presumably, non-Arctic Canadian oil should be considered secure whether imported via land or water.

304. Preferences. The "overland" criterion currently used for exemption from restrictions should be replaced by a judgment based on all the relevant factors: political stability, economic interdependence, and vulnerability to transport interference. It obviously makes no sense to prefer sea shipments from Mexico over Great Lakes shipments from Canada. Caribbean shipments are as secure from transport interference as Gulf Coast shipments and possibly less vulnerable to submarine interdiction than movements by sea from Alaska or the Canadian Arctic islands. On the other hand, there may be reason to consider Canada more reliable than any other foreign supplier — because of present and potential common energy policies and because of the relatively greater assurance that mainly inland oil movements between the two countries will not be diverted to meet foreign deficits in the event of a world supply shortage. The complex of factors to be considered may yield a judgment that a given supplier should be granted complete exemption from restrictions or some qualified form of preference. Whatever the judgment, the preferred or exempt shipments should be treated consistently with the underlying security determination.

335. Canadian preference. (a) Volumes. If either the illustrative intermediate or high tariff were applied to Eastern Hemisphere crude, Canadian oil exports to the United States could be expected to increase substantially by 1980 assuming that only the existing $0.105 per barrel tariff is imposed on Canadian oil. Some of this oil could move to the U.S. East Coast via a trans-Canadian pipeline if one were constructed to transport both Alaskan and Canadian crude, thus reducing East Coast dependence on tanker deliveries.

335b. Security of deliveries. The risk of political instability or animosity is generally conceded to be very low in Canada. The risk of physical interruption or diversion of Canadian oil to other export markets in an emergency is also minimal for those deliveries made by inland transport. And potentially divertible Canadian oil moving by tanker from the Arctic or Atlantic areas could be covered by appropriate intergovernmental arrangements.

335c. Harmonized energy policies. A large U.S. tariff preference for Canadian oil is difficult to justify while Eastern Canada continues to import all of its requirements from potentially insecure sources. In case of a supply interruption, Canada could be expected to turn to the United States to furnish those imports, or to compete for whatever supply is available, and thereby to subtract from the security value of U.S. imports from Western Canada. Some provision for limiting or offsetting Canadian vulnerability to an interruption of its own oil imports should therefore be made a precondition to unrestricted entry of Canadian oil into our market. Full realization of the security benefits implicit in such a preferential arrangement is also dependent on the development of common or harmonized United States-Canadian policies with respect to pipeline and other modes of transportation, access to natural gas, and other related energy matters. Pending the outcome of discussions on these subjects, the United States must decide what arrangements it is prepared to make unilaterally.

336i. Differential treatment of Latin America and Canada. Apart from the excess-imports problem and the difficulties of administering a partial exemption, there are several reasons for differentiating Latin American from Canadian imports. First, of course, is the security of deliverable supplies: If the problem of Eastern Canadian dependence on insecure supplies can be resolved, then Canada will be a more secure source of supply than any Latin American producer. Second, several Latin American countries are both producers and importers of oil; it would probably not be feasible to negotiate an "Eastern Canada" type of solution with each of them, as might have to be done before a full exemption from increased duties could be justified. Third, there are greater prospects for new Canadian discoveries than for discoveries in such countries as Venezuela — a tariff exemption for the former will call forth additional production while one for the latter is not expected to do so. Finally, the economic infrastructure of the United States is and can be far more integrated with that of Canada and perhaps Mexico than with the economy of any other Latin American country; and the possibilities for mutually beneficial coordination of energy policies are greater.

3336j. Conclusion. There are security benefits to be gained from encouraging Latin American as opposed to Eastern Hemisphere imports. To take just one example, a selective boycott against the United States alone by Eastern Hemisphere producers could be deterred by readily available imports from Venezuela. Caribbean imports are also more protectible against submarines. A full tariff exemption, however, would present real difficulties. For present purposes, we propose an initially smaller tariff preference — a reduction of $0.20 per barrel below the Eastern Hemisphere crude tariff, and a $0.30 tariff advantage over the Eastern Hemisphere on residual fuel oil — than is extended to Canadian imports. We further recommend, however, that the question of Latin American preferences be kept under continuing review by the managers of the program, and that careful consideration be given to the possibility of enlarging the preference when the next comprehensive review of the program is conducted as we recommend in the mid-1970's.

343b. Canada. Canada would be permitted to export to the United States as a whole 615,000 b/d of crude or products at existing tariff rates during the first six months of the transition — roughly the volumes expected in July 1970. In each of the two succeeding six-month periods, Canadian imports would be allowed to increase by 15,000 b/d; in the next six-month period these imports could increase by a further 135,000 b/d. At this point — July 1, 1972 — in the intermediate tariff case, all restrictions on imports from Canada except the present $0.105 tariff would be lifted, provided that a mutually satisfactory energy pact had been concluded by then. In the high tariff case, Canadian imports would continue to be restricted for two further six-month periods, but they would be permitted to increase by 120,000 b/d in the first additional period and 50,000 b/d in the second period. These schedules are designed to conform to the anticipated pattern of near-term domestic production as prorationing restraints are removed, and to avoid excessive fluctuations in the share of the market left open for Eastern Hemisphere imports. The bulk of the scheduled increases would come into Districts I-IV; Canadian imports into District V would be allowed to increase up to the capacity of existing pipelines during the period of volumetric controls. All of these imports would pay only the existing tariff. Rights to these imports of Canadian crude or products into Districts I-IV would either be auctioned to refiners in those districts or allocated uniformly to them on the basis of refinery inputs. Such rights could then be resold under a mandatory exchange or disclosure system but only to importers in Districts I-IV.

425. Conclusion. National security will be adequately protected by adopting as a first step a revised control system and a modest immediate reduction in import restraints. Further liberalization appears to be warranted, but a decision on the timing and extent of subsequent relaxation in the level of restrictions should await the development of additional information about the productive potential of North American "frontier areas." A prudent course, in other words, would be to adopt a system of tariff restrictions, to take effect no later than January 1, 1971, at an approximate level of $1.45 per barrel ($1.35 above existing tariffs) and to allot the balance of 1970 and 1971 for collection and evaluation of confirmatory information. This would have the additional advantage of allowing the new control system to prove itself in operation. If the program managers are persuaded — on the basis of objective and independent professional appraisal of actual exploratory drilling and other then-current information — that indicated reserves in North American frontier areas will be sufficient to meet or exceed the aggregate 1980 production estimates set forth in this report, a schedule of further tariff liberalization should be announced and put into effect by January of 1972. If no tariff liberalization is undertaken in 1972, the same test should be applied in succeeding Januaries until there occurs a full review of the program, which should in any event be carried out no later than 1975.

427b. Specific preferences. In our judgment, Canadian and Mexican oil is nearly as secure politically and militarily as our own, although complete realization of these security benefits will require fully understood and harmonized energy policies. We therefore recommend that, after an appropriate transition, Canadian and Mexican imports be exempt from the program, if common energy accords can be arranged with those governments.

Because oil from other Western Hemisphere sources has been delivered without interruption over the years, we consider that imports from those areas should be treated preferentially. An initial full exemption would be unworkable, although it could become feasible by or shortly after the end of the decade. We therefore recommend that crude oil and refinery products including residual fuel oil from Western Hemisphere sources other than Canada and Mexico receive preference in the form of lower tariffs. We also recommend that careful consideration be given, no later than the mid-1970's review of the program, to possible future widening of this preference.

SEPARATE REPORT

I. Effectiveness of Present Oil Import Program

The National Security

The preeminent position of the United States in the world depends in large part on the uninterrupted flow of oil and its products to its armed forces and civilian economy. The total domestic demand for oil, which was 9.5 million barrels per day (b/d) in 1959, and is presently in excess of 13.5 million b/d, is growing steadily and under present conditions will probably exceed 19 million b/d by 1980 and 23 million b/d by 1985.

In an emergency there are generally no practical substitutes for oil, and normal petroleum consumption cannot be reduced by more than a negligible amount without seriously impairing transportation, industrial production, and military capabilities. Such alternatives as using underground storage or surface tanks to store massive reserves are not economically sensible and would require large investments of appropriated government money.

The U.S. is, for the most part, a high-cost producer of oil. If not restricted, imports of lower-cost oil would enter in such volume as to destroy much of the existing crude oil producing industry of the U.S. in the next decade. This would render the nation heavily dependent on foreign production and would pose a demonstrable threat to the national security unless such production were certain to be available under any conditions.

President Nixon recognized the threat to the national security by uncertainty of oil supplies in his press conference of September 26, 1969, when he said, ". . . I believe it is essential to develop all our resources when, as we look at the Middle East and other sections of the world, many of our supplies could be cut off in the event of a world conflict."

The measure of this risk is clearly demonstrated by the estimate provided for the record by one major producer to the effect that, if tariff or quota action is taken to force the price of crude oil to $2.50 a barrel, the United States would have to import 14 million b/d from Eastern Hemisphere countries in 1985 to meet its then total requirements of 25.6 million b/d (including 2.2 million b/d to meet the natural gas deficit). Clearly, the national security would not be protected under such conditions.

IV. Alternative Plan for Revision of the Mandatory Oil Import Program

A. Summary of Alternative Plan

(1) Maintain for the present the three established geographical districts currently in use under the Mandatory Oil Import Program.

(2) Provide additional imports of foreign petroleum into Districts I-IV for each of the five years from 1970 through 1974 by increasing the present import quota formula (12.2%) for these districts by the equivalent of one percentage point in each year. Adjust the formula, however, to relate imports to inputs instead of to production as at present.

(3) Continue unrestricted entry of residual fuel oil into District I, and consider extending this privilege also to the other districts. Encourage domestic production of low sulphur residual fuel oil.

(4)(a) Negotiate with Canada toward a common energy policy which would provide secure supplies of oil and gas to the United States and which would cover all energy sources. In the meantime, continue an arrangement with Canada, but on an effective basis of restraint that would provide for reasonable annual growth in imports from that country.

(b) Encourage Mexico to discontinue its 30,000 b/d quota, in view of that country's limited supply.

(5) Phase out within two to three years the present crude oil allocations to refiners based on historical imports.

(6) Retain the sliding scale preference for the smaller refineries.

(7) Provide petrochemical producers with a growing volume of imported oil.

(8) Phase out within three years historical import allocations for finished products. Provide import allocations of No. 2 heating oil for terminal operators in District I on a basis equal to that allowed to oil refiners.

(9) Continue the existing formula for oil imports into District V, with minor changes, pending determination of the quantity and availability of North Slope Alaskan production.

(10) Permit unrestricted entry of foreign oil into foreign trade zones for manufacture for export.

(11) Reject future special arrangements favoring individual companies that have been established in Puerto Rico and the Virgin Islands.

(12) Clarify the authority of the Oil Import Appeals Board, but confine its responsibility to problems of individual companies.

(13) Continue administration of the Oil Import Program under the Department of the Interior, with policy recommendations made by a Policy Committee consisting essentially of the present agency members of the Task Force. Review oil import policy broadly again at the Cabinet level in 1973 or 1974.

(14) Provide incentives to encourage imports of crude and unfinished oils and residual fuel oil from Western Hemisphere producing countries.

iii Greene Address

from text of an address by the Hon. J. J. Greene, Minister of Energy, Mines and Resources, Canada, to the Mid-year Meeting of the Independent Petroleum Association of America. Denver, Colorado, May 12, 1970.

We were ready to talk with your government earlier this year. Indeed discussions between officials regarding the scope and nature of future energy talks had already started when the wrench of arbitrary import controls was thrown into the machinery of negotiation.

This stopped all activity for some weeks, but we have recently had an approach from your government to resume talks. However, a situation in which a large part of our exports are under control represents a less-than-ideal environment in which to hold discussions. For this reason, it is difficult for me to be precise as to timing of talks. The unilateral action on quotas has created for us grave political problems which I am very sure were not considered by U.S. officials who recommended the arbitrary shut-off and restrictions. Canadian public opinion is interpreting this as a pressure play, to squeeze Canada into some form of energy deal which would not be to the Canadian advantage.

Prime Minister Trudeau has described living next door to the U.S. to be a little like sleeping with a friendly elephant. Canadians interpret the unilateral oil cut back as the elephant rolling over on top of the poor Canadian mouse. A physical condition which is not only uncomfortable but a difficult posture for the mouse, from which to begin long-term energy discussions.

When the time *does* come to sit down with representatives of your government, we shall want to find out more about what they have in mind with regard to an energy deal, and what arrangements can be achieved which are in the Canadian interest and yet of benefit to the United States.

What we seek are realistic trading arrangements in respect of oil which would secure that Canadian oil enters United States markets on a normal commercial basis.

I recognize that this simple goal may prove difficult of attainment. But I am confident as to ultimate success because I believe that such an outcome would be entirely consistent with the basic complementarity of resources and requirements in the two countries and the mutual benefit of our two peoples.

Supply Security of Canadian Oil

The matter of supply security is going to come up in any negotiations regarding access for Canadian oil to U.S. markets.

Concerns have been expressed in the Shultz report and, orally, by American officials, that dependence of eastern Canada on imported oil carries unfavourable implications for the security of deliveries to eastern Canada and to the U.S. in conditions of world oil supply emergency.

Specifically, there have been suggestions that in an emergency western Canadian oil might be diverted from U.S. markets to meet needs in eastern Canada if adequate tanker-borne supplies were not available to that area.

Secondly, it has been suggested that the U.S. would have to be prepared to make emergency deliveries of its domestic oil to eastern Canada if overseas supplies to the whole eastern seaboard of North America were curtailed.

As to the security of our export deliveries to United States markets, this has surely never been seriously challenged. Indeed, the work of the U.S. Cabinet Task Force on oil import control tended, if anything, to confirm the reliability of Canadian supply. Diversion to eastern Canadian markets of oil flowing to the U.S. would not at present be possible because of the absence of the necessary pipe line connections. And having regard to the long standing arrangements between our two countries in defence, trade and other areas, I cannot find it credible that we would divert such supplies unless by mutual agreement for a common purpose or that we would violate trading agreements that were in effect between us.

As to the question of supply of U.S. domestic oil to eastern Canadian markets in crisis conditions, some movements took place during the Suez crises of 1956-57 and 1967. However, we shall point out to your government that the additional Canadian supply made available to U.S. west coast refineries exceeded by a large margin the emergency deliveries we received from you in the east.

This is not to say that we are complacent as to the matter of eastern Canadian oil supply security.

Hitherto, we have not considered the danger of supply interruption to be such as to require revision of our policy. But there are changing circumstances and we have this question under careful examination in the context of our review of national oil policy.

If we conclude that a problem exists, then we shall seek to apply solutions appropriate to Canadian circumstances. These might include storage in eastern Canada, arrangements to exchange Canadian for U.S. oil in an emergency or the supply of some western Canadian oil to our eastern provinces. A complete answer could, of course, come with discovery of large oil resources on the Atlantic Shelf or in the Canadian Arctic.

In these circumstances it must be left to *us*, to Canada, to evaluate the matter of oil supply security in eastern Canada and to take any appropriate action. I am convinced that the solutions which will prove to best serve our joint interests will be those very solutions we come to as being the Canadian solutions in the Canadian interest.

This aspect of freedom of domestic policy-making is most important to us. We believe our national and international, political and economic circumstances are such that we must retain freedom to apply Canadian solutions to Canadian problems. This is an important consideration entering into any discussions we may have with your government regarding long term arrangements on oil. The Canadian people would not tolerate decisions affecting Canadian security being made at the insistence of non-Canadians, even to win in the prize of larger oil markets.

NATURAL GAS

One Canadian energy commodity which is likely to face minimal obstacles on importation to the U.S. is natural gas.

The U.S. faces a difficult, some would claim critical, supply-demand situation in respect of natural gas.

We in Canada have established a substantial natural gas resource base. And the potential for this hydrocarbon is expected to match that of oil. Supply which has been declared surplus to domestic needs by both federal and provincial authorities is available for export.

Any such surplus is likely to be very readily absorbed in the U.S. market. And there are clear indications your government and the Federal Power Commission would like to see steps taken to accelerate the volume of Canadian supply available to the U.S.

This is a far cry from the situation of a few years ago when the Energy Board and your F.P.C. were at considerably more than arms's length on this matter.

I believe your Association's policy was to recommend restriction of Canadian gas imports to a fixed proportion of total U.S. supply. I think your position here had considerably less to commend it than the line you have taken on Canadian oil imports.

Our National Energy Board currently has before it applications for licences for further large export volumes. At the same time the Board is reviewing the criteria used to satisfy itself, as by Statute it must, that the quantity of gas to be exported is surplus to reasonably foreseeable requirements for use in Canada.

This matter being *sub judice* it would be improper for me to comment further. I would, however, make two points.

First, viewed against the scale of United States needs, Canadian gas resources likely to be available for export presently appear relatively small. To illustrate: Based on resources in the western Canada sedimentary basin, we might have about 1.6 trillion cubic feet available for export in 1990, not much more than double the current annual volume. I feel it would be wrong for your industry and your policy makers, if they were so tempted, to look to Canadian supplies as a panacea for the ills of the American natural gas industry.

Secondly, Canadian gas will be available to supplement United States supplies only if our petroleum industry as a whole receives the incentives of progressive growth and assured stability of access to export markets for oil and natural gas liquids. Should this happen, it has been estimated that the western Canada sedimentary basin supplemented by our frontier areas, could supply as much as 5.4 trillion cubic feet to export in 1990.

TAX POLICY

This matter of incentives is very important. I'm convinced of the need for appropriate investment climates to secure the objective of maintaining a vigorous, innovating petroleum industry to make the best use of our resources. And tax policy is, of course, an important element in such climates.

All of you who have interests in Canada will be aware that our government has made public proposals for tax reform. These are being studied closely and debated vigorously. The government has determined that a thorough overhaul of our whole tax system is required, one which will touch nearly every personal and corporate taxpayer. The petroleum industry is not the least of the affected parties.

This matter of tax reform is outside the immediate scope of my portfolio. But I would judge it unlikely that in implementing its proposals government would ride roughshod over the petroleum industry's best interests. In particular, I cannot see that it would legislate a tax climate in which the Canadian petroleum industry would be put at any significantly increased disadvantage compared with the industry in the U.S.

Which takes me to another aspect of our relationships in the petroleum industry, and at the same time to the doorway of the broader aspects of the relations between our two countries. This is the question of foreign ownership of Canadian resource and other industries. We have already adopted laws which assure the ownership by Canadians of our commercial banks, federally incorporated trust, loan, and insurance companies, our radio and television industry and our newspapers.

We have recently determined that a major proportion of a resource essential to our future well-being, uranium, will remain in Canadian hands. We are currently undertaking a complete review of foreign ownership of our resource and industrial entities. I feel very certain that if, in America, some 70 per cent of your petroleum industry and some 60 per cent of your natural resources, and some 50 per cent of your manufacturing industry was owned by non-Americans, you would share an equal concern. The problem of the absentee landlord was that which kept that wonderful, yet apparently ill-starred isle of Ireland in turmoil not only over the years, but almost centuries.

We are fully aware that a good proportion of our economic well-being is founded on the savings of the people of other lands, largely American, who have invested in Canada and formed the basis of our economic growth. We are not unmindful of the fact that much of our well-being stems from this bounty, but Canadians are now determined that the time has come to take stock and to assure that a substantial proportion of the future growth remains in Canadian hands.

This is at least in part because of the changing nature of the basic unit of the world of business. The basic unit of the future will likely be the conglomerate having a national home, but engaging in multi-national business in the open marketplaces of the world.

If a country does not participate at sources, does not assure that these new business giants are domiciled at home, such a country will become essentially a branch plant economy, with attendant diminution of opportunity for its young people. Canadians are determined to participate to the full in the tomorrows, and give to their gifted and able young people the opportunity to participate as Canadians, in Canadian entities, which will compete in this new kind of business world. This opportunity will not exist unless we make those determinations now, which will assure a greater Canadian control of our own industries and resources.

Yet, there is no question but that we shall require continuing and increasing sources of investment capital from abroad, if we are to maintain a satisfactory rate of economic growth. We are convinced that this can be accomplished by rules which will achieve a greater and growing proportion of Canadian ownership and still provide a just return to the foreign investor.

NOTES

CHAPTER I
1. *The Globe and Mail,* Aug. 12, 1970.
2. *Ibid.,* July 26, 1970.
3. *Toronto Star,* Aug. 11, 1970.
4. *The Globe and Mail,* Aug. 14, 1970.
5. *Ibid.,* June 24, 1970
6. *Ibid.,* June 24, 1970.
7. Canada, National Energy Board, *Energy Supply and Demand in Canada and Export Demand for Canadian Energy, 1966, to 1990,* Ottawa, 1969, p. 61.
8. *Ibid.,* p. 56.
9. *Ibid.,* p. 19.
10. Royal Society of Canada, *Water Resources of Canada,* (Toronto, 1967), p. 23.
11. *Toronto Star,* May 29, 1970.
12. Greene, J. J., *Address to the Mid-Year Meeting of the Independent Petroleum Association of America, Denver Colorado,* (mimeographed by the Department of Energy, Mines and Resources, Ottawa, 1970), p. 31.
13. *Ibid.,* p. 34.
14. *Ibid.,* p. 36.
15. *Ibid.,* p. 19.
16. *Ibid.,* p. 20.
17. *Ibid.,* p. 21.
18. *Ibid.,* p. 24.
19. *Ibid.,* p. 25.
20. *Ibid.,* p. 26.
21. *Ibid.,* p. 28.
22. United States Information Service, *Canadian-American Relations, 1867-1967,* (Ottawa, 1967), v. I, p. 44.
23. *Ibid.,* p. 41.
24. *Ibid.,* p. 36.
25. *Ibid.,* pp. 38,39.
26. *Ibid.,* p. 38.
27. *The Globe and Mail,* June 23, 1970.
28. *Financial Post,* Aug. 8, 1970.
29. *The Globe and Mail,* June 25, 1970.
30. *Ibid.,* July 9, 1970.
31. *Ibid.,* Feb. 4, 1970.
32. *Petroleum Today,* Summer 1969.
33. *Ibid.,* Winter 1969.
34. Dominion Bureau of Statistics, *Canada Year Book 1968,* (Ottawa, 1969), p. 928.

CHAPTER II
1. Innis, Harold, *The Fur Trade in Canada,* (Toronto, 1962), p. 385.
2. Dominion Bureau of Statistics, *Canadian Statistical Review,* May, 1970, pp. 105, 106.
3. *Ibid.,* p. 107.

4. Adelman, M. A., *Oil Production Costs in Four Areas,* 1966, quoted in Penrose, Edith T., *The Large International Firm in Developing Countries: The International Petroleum Industry,* (London, 1968), p. 195.
5. *The Oil Import Question, A report on the Relationship of Oil Imports to the National Security,* (Washington, 1970), p. 22.
6. *Ibid.,* p. 19.
7. *Ibid.,* p. 297.
8. Dominion Bureau of Statistics, *Canada Year Book 1968,* (Ottawa, 1969), p. 1037.
9. Dominion Bureau of Statistics, *1967 Corporation Taxation Statistics,* (Ottawa, 1968).
10. Gonick, C. W., *"Foreign Ownership and Political Decay",* from Lumsden, C. I. (ed.), *Close the 49th Parallel Etc.,* (Toronto, 1970), p. 65.
11. Baran, Paul, Sweezy, Paul, *Monopoly Capital,* (New York, 1964), pp. 195, 196.
12. *Financial Post,* July 11, 1970.
13. Dominion Bureau of Statistics, *Inter-Corporate Ownership 1965,* (Ottawa, 1969).
14. *Canadian Forum,* July-August 1970.

CHAPTER III
1. Kolko, Gabriel, *The Roots of American Foreign Policy,* (Boston, 1969), p. 51.
2. *Resources for Freedom, The Outlook for Energy Sources,* v. III, (Washington, 1952), p. 6.
3. *Fortune,* August 1969.
4. Godfrey Dave, and Watkins, Mel, (ed), *Gordon to Watkins to You,* (Toronto, 1970), p. 142.
5. Shaffer, Edward H., *The Oil Import Program of the United States,* (New York, 1968), p. 18.
6. *Ibid.,* p. 109.
7. *Ibid.,* p. 110.
8. *Ibid.,* p. 129.
9. *Ibid.,* p. 122.
10. *Ibid.,* p. 213.
11. *Ibid.,* p. 215.
12. *The Oil Import Question,* p. 31.
13. *Ibid.,* p. 126.
14. *Ibid.,* p. 57.
15. *Ibid.,* p. 94.
16. *Ibid.,* p. 335.
17. *Ibid.,* p. 105.
18. *Ibid.,* p. 354.
19. Greene, J. J., *Op. Cit.* p. 18.
20. *The Oil Import Question,* p. 43.
21. *Ibid.,* p. 98.
22. *Ibid.,* p. 345.
23. *Ibid.,* p. 362.
24. Kolko, Gabriel, *Op. Cit.,* p. 82.

CHAPTER IV
1. Wright, Jim, *The Coming Water Famine,* (New York, 1966), pp. 219, 220.
2. *Ibid.,* pp. 221, 222.

3. *Ibid.,* pp. 218, 219.
4. *Water Resources of Canada,* pp. 19, 20, 22, 24.
5. *Foreign Affairs,* July 1970, p. 731.
6. *Ibid.,* p. 733.
7. Higgins, Larratt, "The alienation of Canadian resources: the case of the Columbia River Treaty", from Lumsden, C.I. (ed.), *Close the 49th Parallel Etc.,* (Toronto, 1970), p. 225.
8. *Ibid.,* p. 226.
9. *Ibid.,* p. 236.
10. *Ibid.,* p. 238.
11. United States Information Service, *Op. Cit.,* p. 112.
12. Higgins, Larratt, *Op. Cit.,* p. 239.
13. *Toronto Star,* Feb. 25, 1970.
14. *The Globe and Mail,* Feb. 25, 1970.
15. *Ibid.,* July 20, 1970.

CHAPTER V
1. *The Globe and Mail,* July 29, 1970.
2. Baran and Sweezy, *Op. Cit.,* p. 184.
3. *Ibid.,* p. 201.